Jesus
and the Devil

by Jennie Breeden

ISBN:9781534759336
Printed in USA

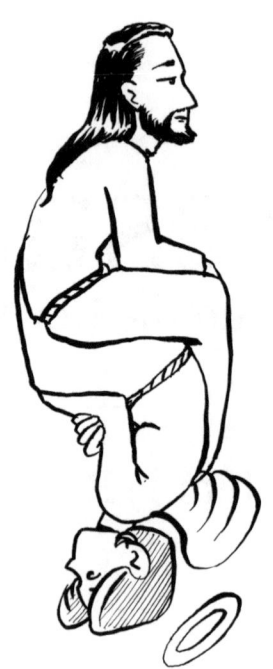

www.TheDevilsPanties.com

A semi autobiographical webcomic about life, the universe, and everything. This is a compilation of the comics where Jesus or the Devil show up.

I think the man had some great ideas.

His fanclub makes me nervouse.

"A person is smart. People are dumb, panicky, dangerous animals, and you know it!"
-Agent K, 'Men in Black'

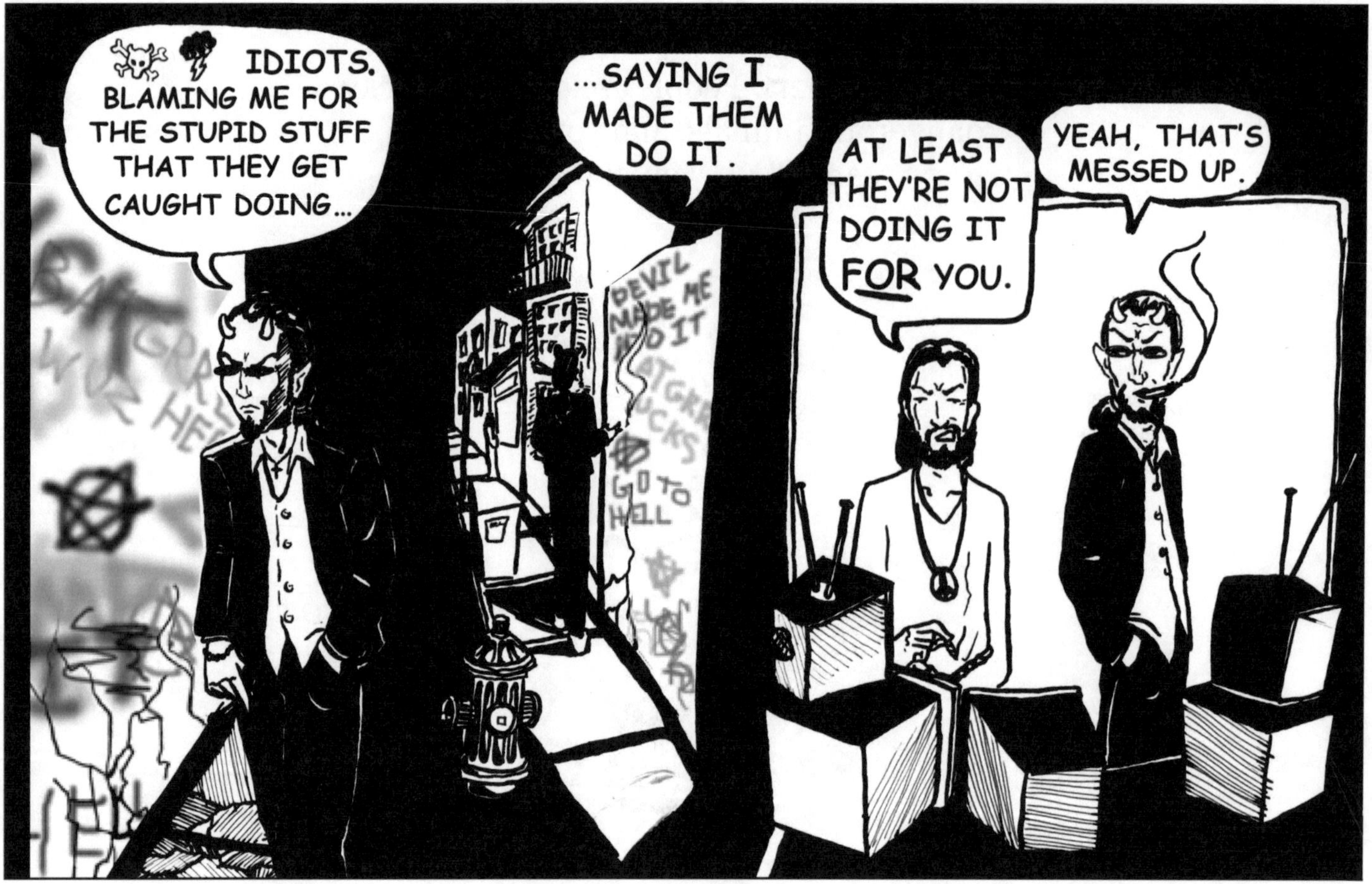
IDIOTS. BLAMING ME FOR THE STUPID STUFF THAT THEY GET CAUGHT DOING...
...SAYING I MADE THEM DO IT.
DEVIL MADE ME DO IT
GO TO HELL
AT LEAST THEY'RE NOT DOING IT FOR YOU.
YEAH, THAT'S MESSED UP.

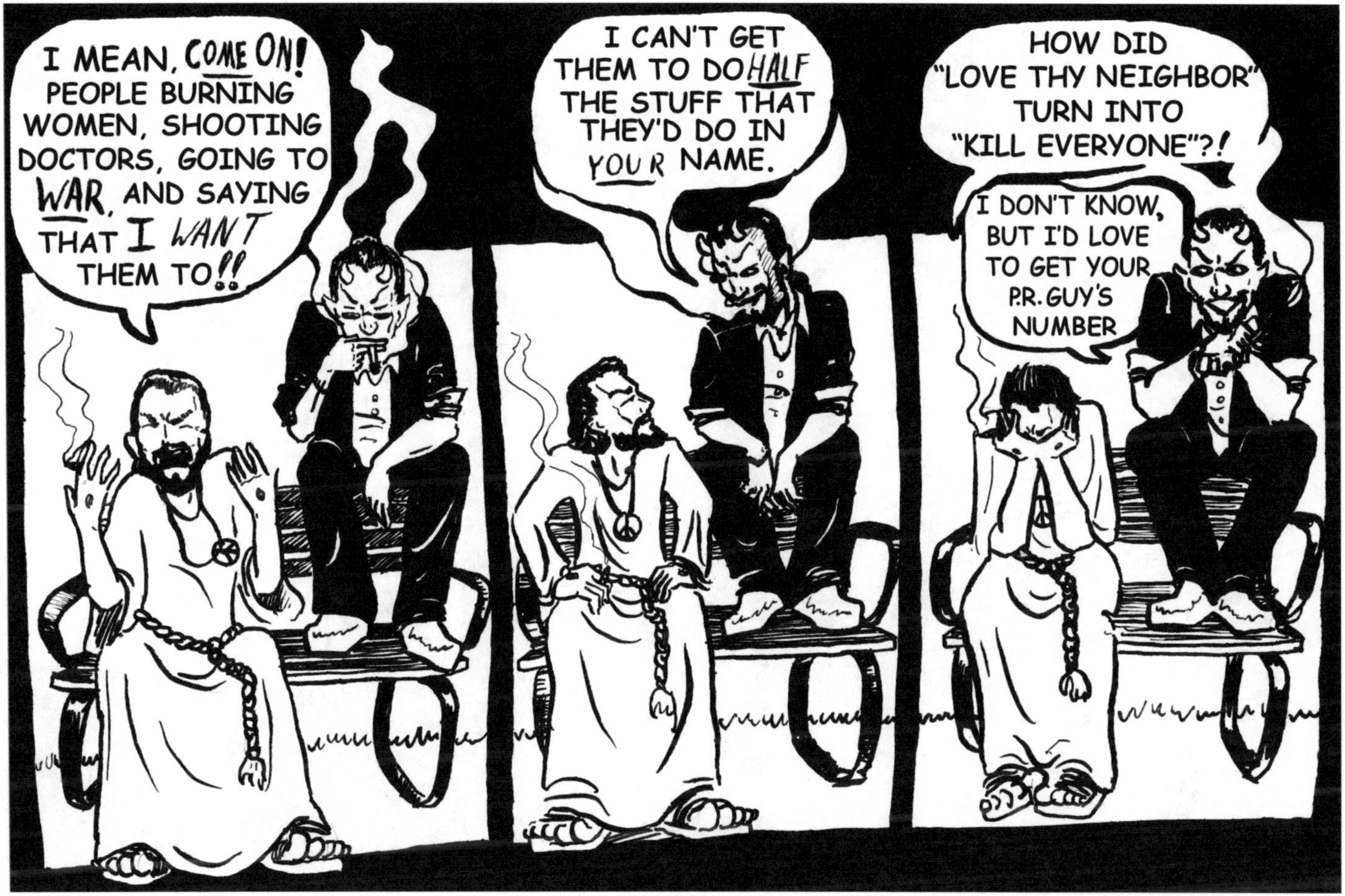
I MEAN, COME ON! PEOPLE BURNING WOMEN, SHOOTING DOCTORS, GOING TO WAR, AND SAYING THAT I WANT THEM TO!!
I CAN'T GET THEM TO DO HALF THE STUFF THAT THEY'D DO IN YOUR NAME.
HOW DID "LOVE THY NEIGHBOR" TURN INTO "KILL EVERYONE"?!
I DON'T KNOW, BUT I'D LOVE TO GET YOUR P.R. GUY'S NUMBER

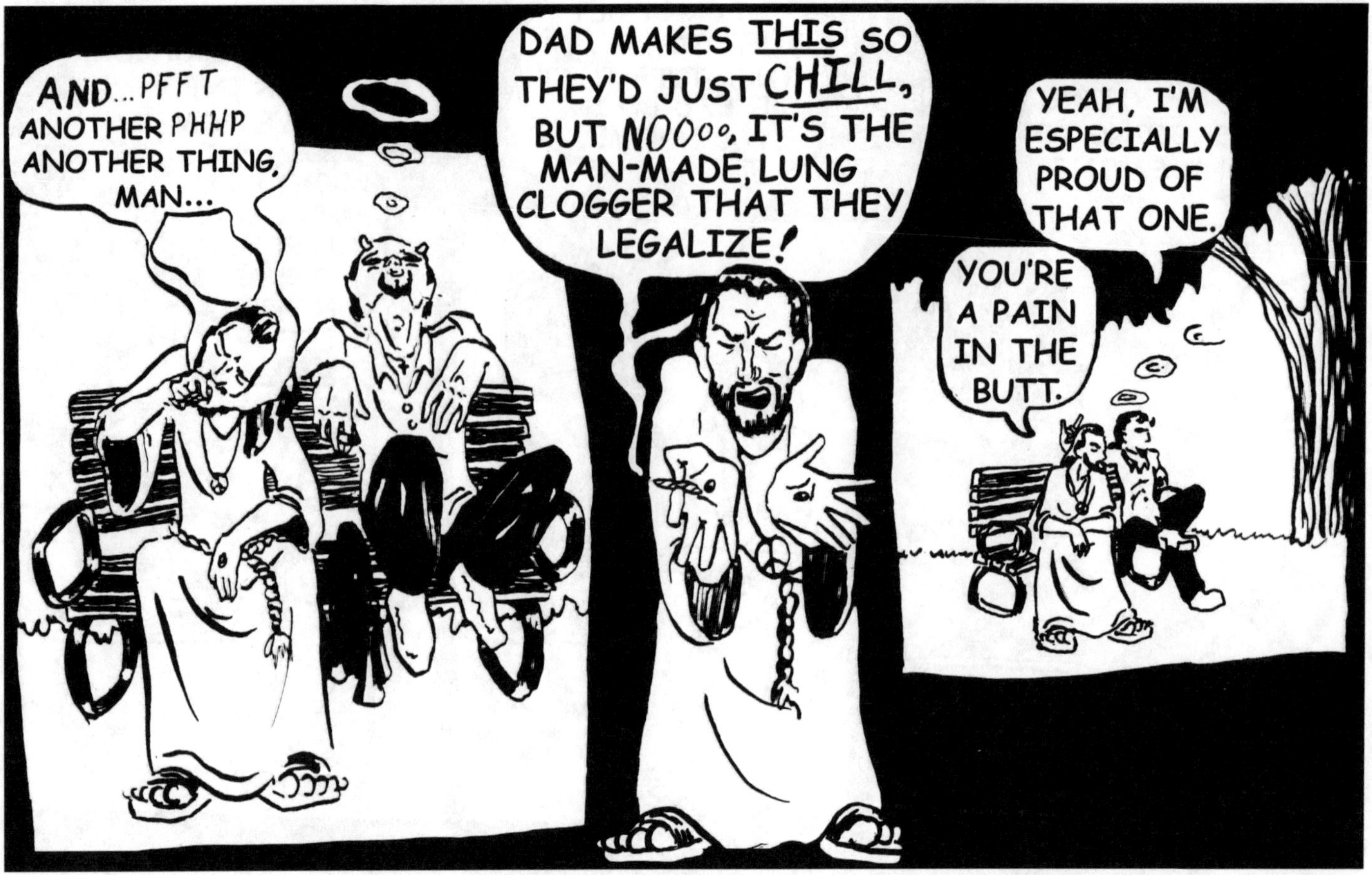
AND... PFFT ANOTHER PHHP ANOTHER THING, MAN...
DAD MAKES THIS SO THEY'D JUST CHILL, BUT NOOoo, IT'S THE MAN-MADE, LUNG CLOGGER THAT THEY LEGALIZE!
YEAH, I'M ESPECIALLY PROUD OF THAT ONE.
YOU'RE A PAIN IN THE BUTT.

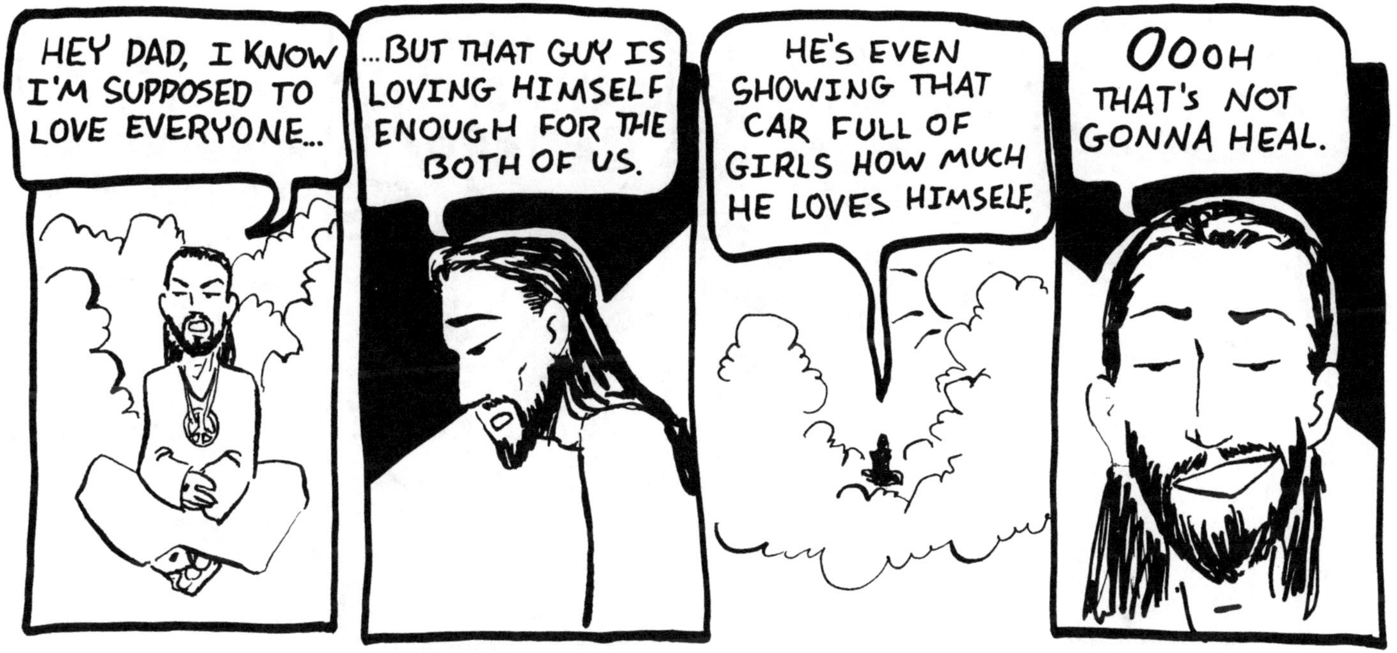
HEY DAD, I KNOW I'M SUPPOSED TO LOVE EVERYONE...
...BUT THAT GUY IS LOVING HIMSELF ENOUGH FOR THE BOTH OF US.
HE'S EVEN SHOWING THAT CAR FULL OF GIRLS HOW MUCH HE LOVES HIMSELF.
OOoH THAT'S NOT GONNA HEAL.

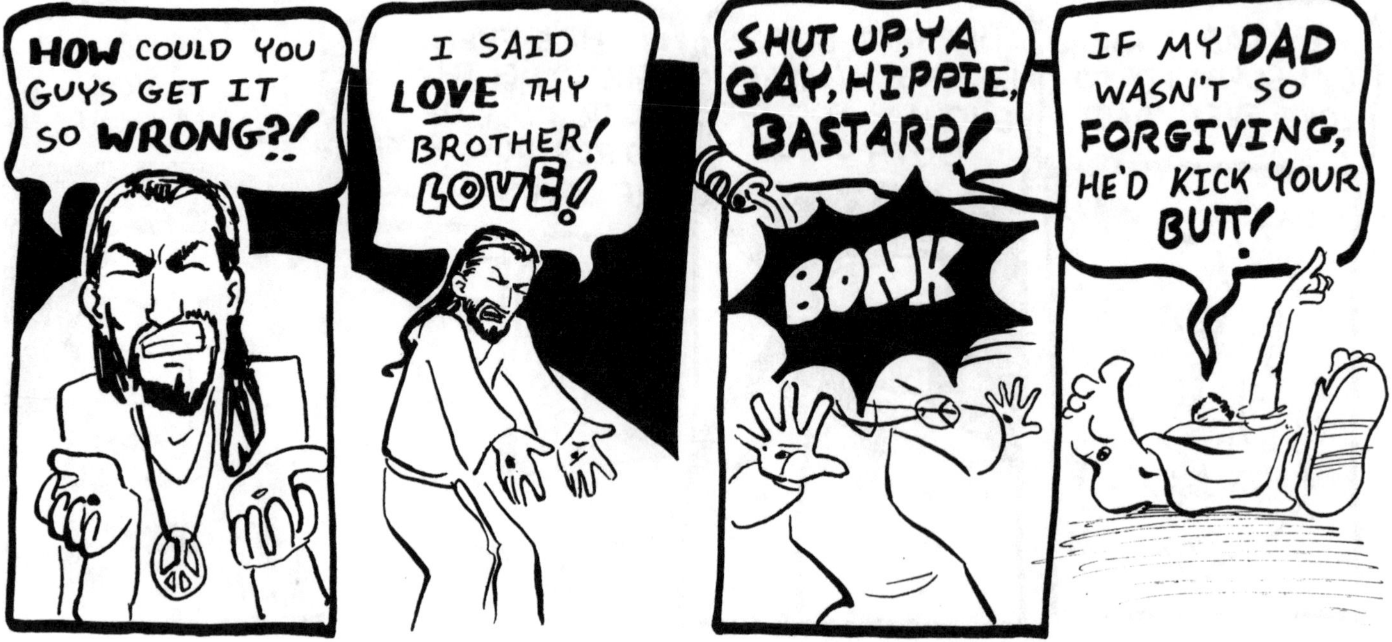
HOW COULD YOU GUYS GET IT SO WRONG?!
I SAID LOVE THY BROTHER! LOVE!
SHUT UP, YA GAY, HIPPIE, BASTARD!
BONK
IF MY DAD WASN'T SO FORGIVING, HE'D KICK YOUR BUTT!

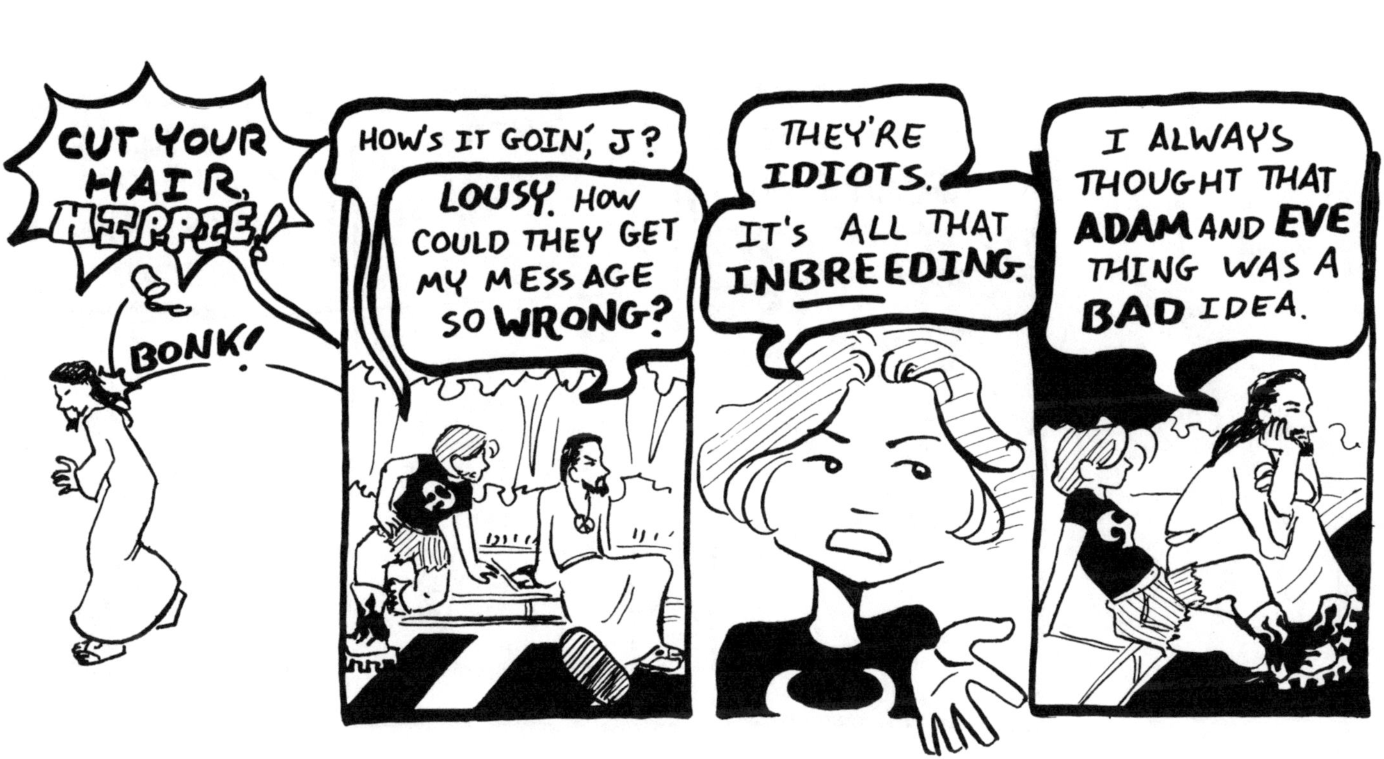
CUT YOUR HAIR, HIPPIE!
BONK!
HOW'S IT GOIN', J?
LOUSY. HOW COULD THEY GET MY MESSAGE SO WRONG?
THEY'RE IDIOTS.
IT'S ALL THAT INBREEDING.
I ALWAYS THOUGHT THAT ADAM AND EVE THING WAS A BAD IDEA.

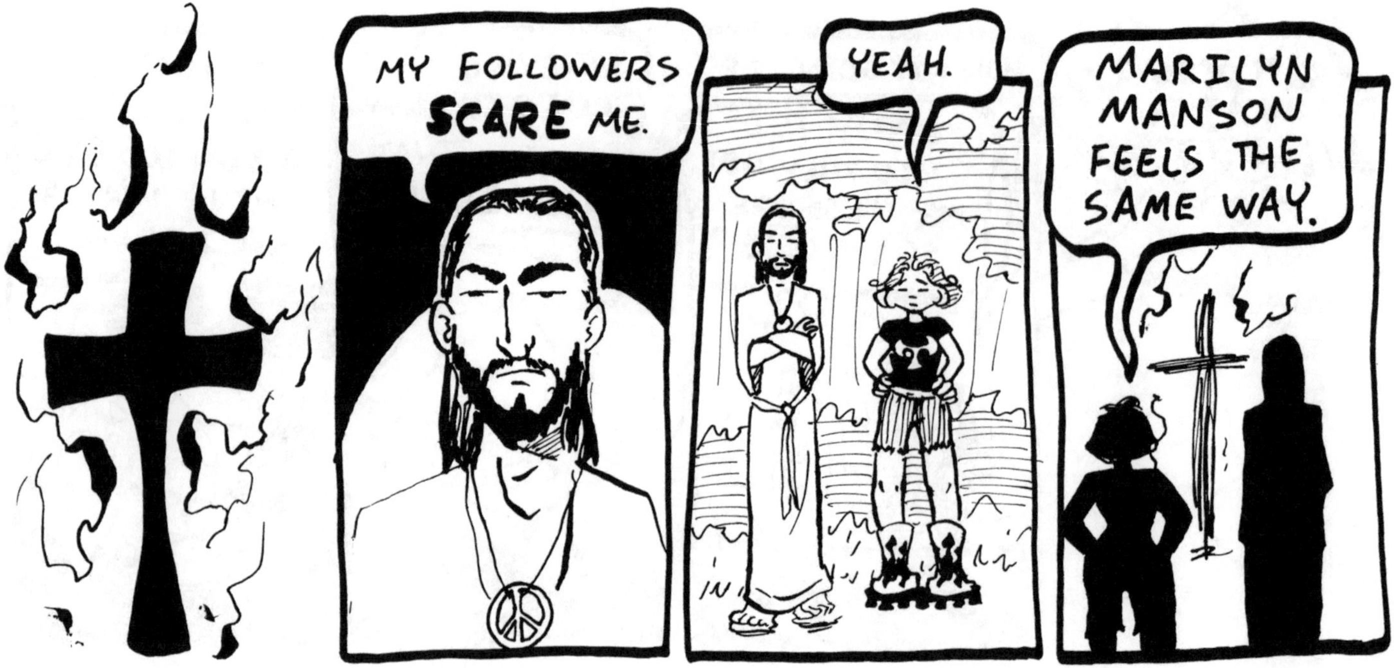
MY FOLLOWERS **SCARE** ME.
YEAH.
MARILYN MANSON FEELS THE SAME WAY.

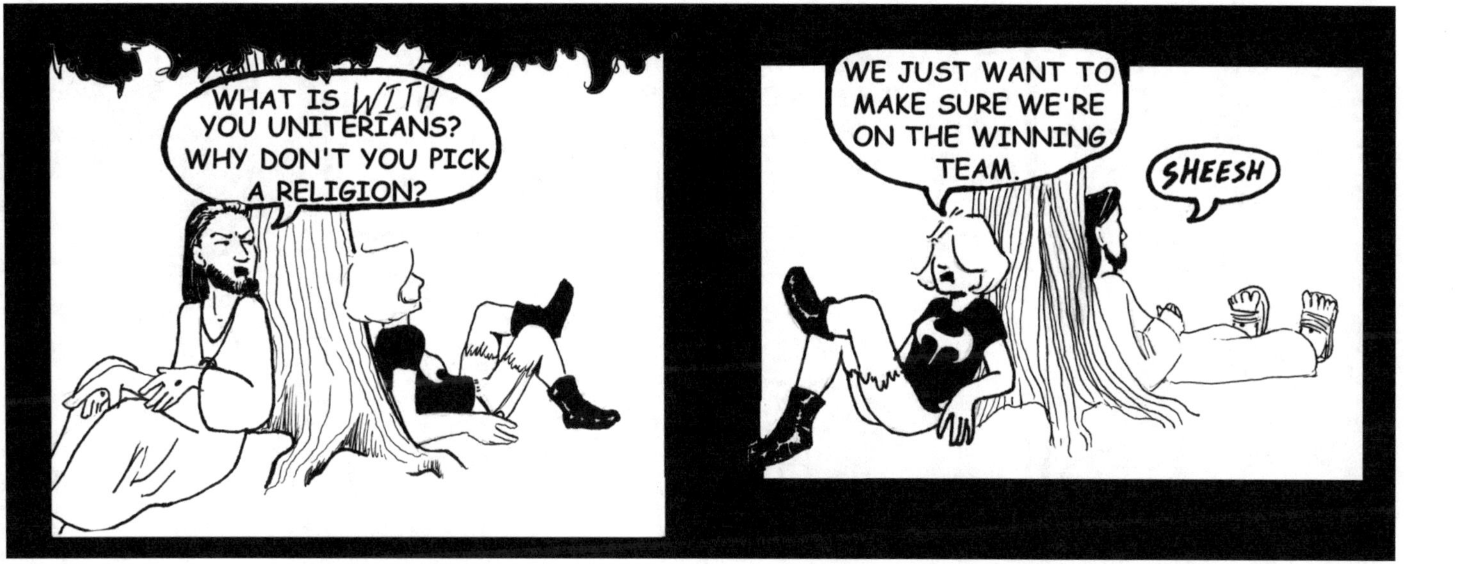
WHAT IS WITH YOU UNITERIANS? WHY DON'T YOU PICK A RELIGION?
WE JUST WANT TO MAKE SURE WE'RE ON THE WINNING TEAM.
SHEESH

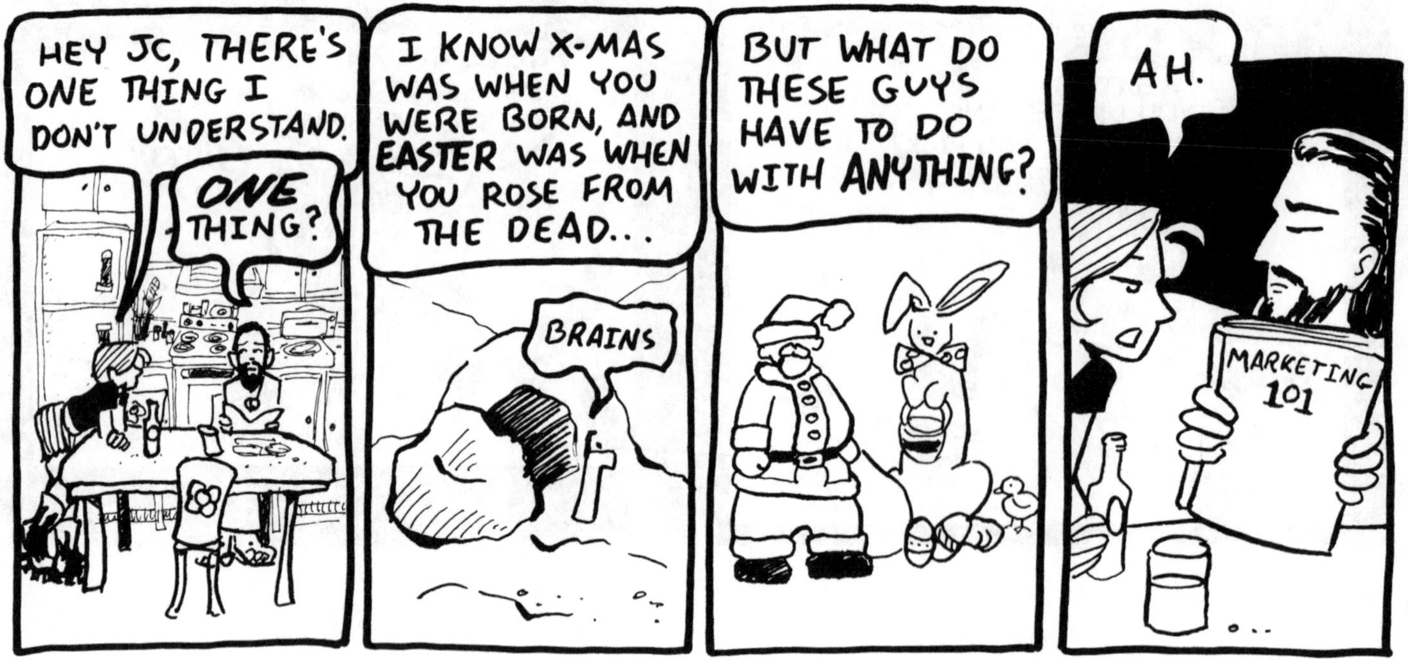
HEY JC, THERE'S ONE THING I DON'T UNDERSTAND.
ONE THING?
I KNOW X-MAS WAS WHEN YOU WERE BORN, AND EASTER WAS WHEN YOU ROSE FROM THE DEAD...
BRAINS
BUT WHAT DO THESE GUYS HAVE TO DO WITH ANYTHING?
AH.
MARKETING 101
...

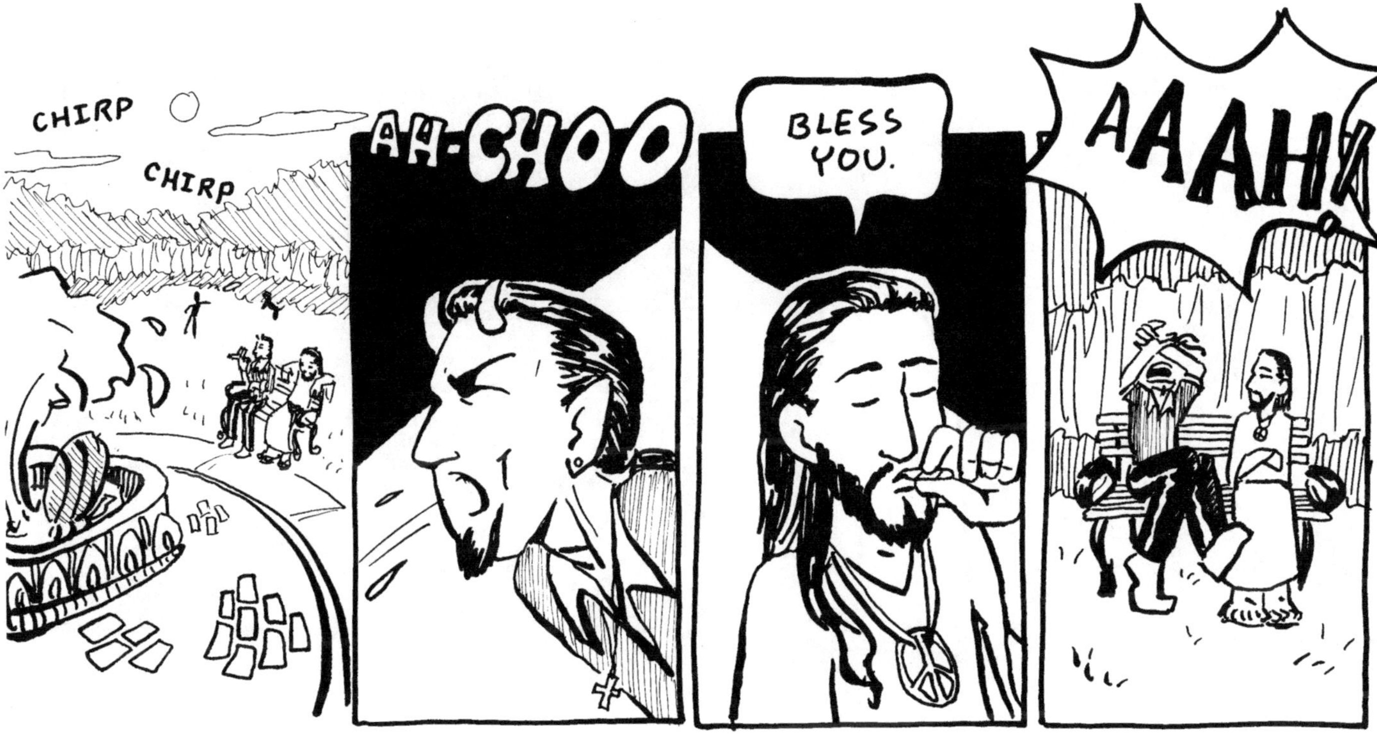
CHIRP
CHIRP
AH-CHOO
BLESS YOU.
AAAH!

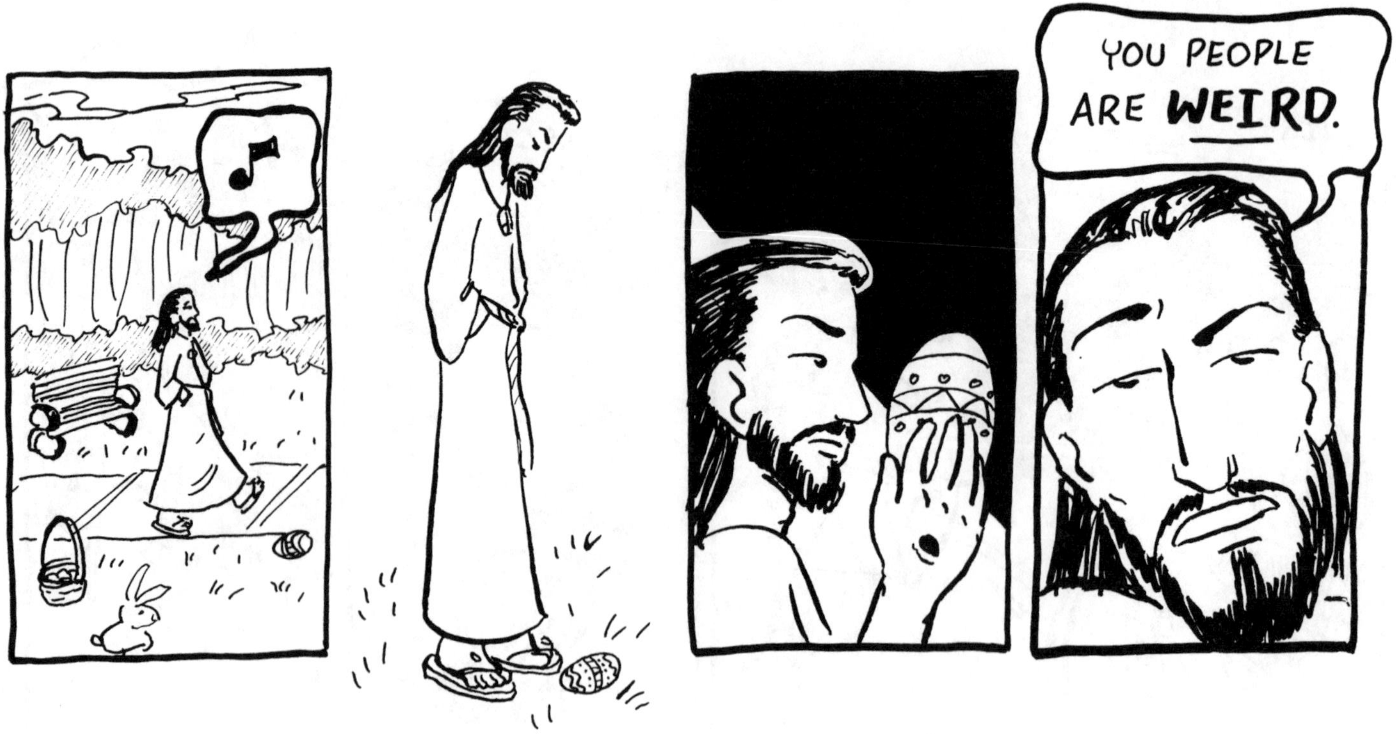
YOU PEOPLE ARE WEIRD.

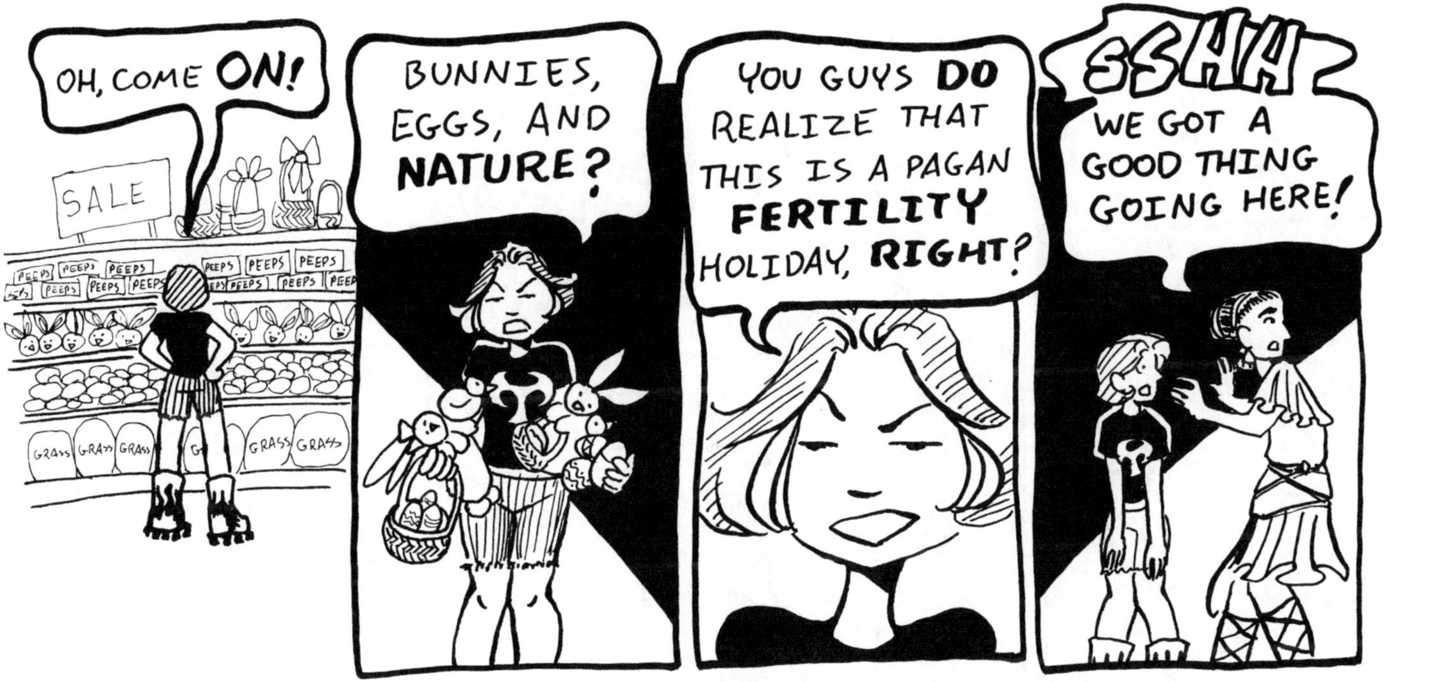
OH, COME ON!
SALE
PEEPS
GRASS
BUNNIES, EGGS, AND NATURE?
YOU GUYS DO REALIZE THAT THIS IS A PAGAN FERTILITY HOLIDAY, RIGHT?
SSHH
WE GOT A GOOD THING GOING HERE!

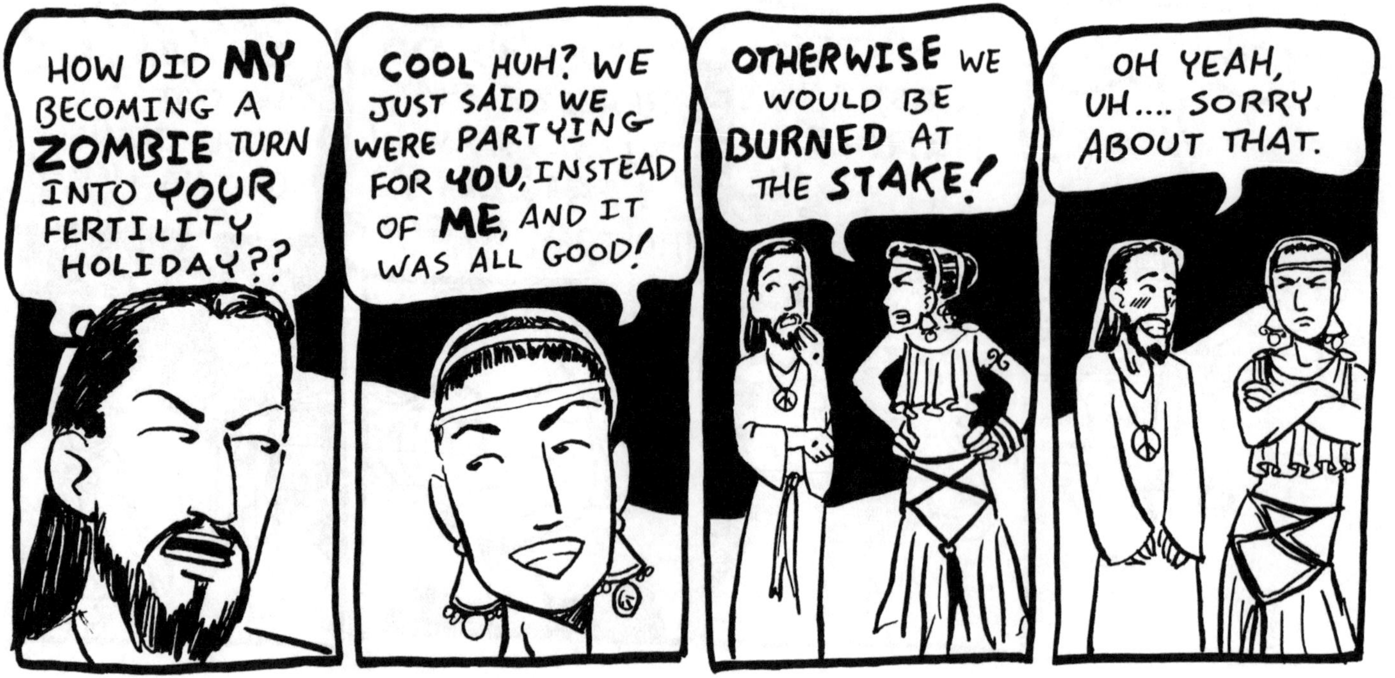
HOW DID MY BECOMING A ZOMBIE TURN INTO YOUR FERTILITY HOLIDAY??
COOL HUH? WE JUST SAID WE WERE PARTYING FOR YOU, INSTEAD OF ME, AND IT WAS ALL GOOD!
OTHERWISE WE WOULD BE BURNED AT THE STAKE!
OH YEAH, UH.... SORRY ABOUT THAT.

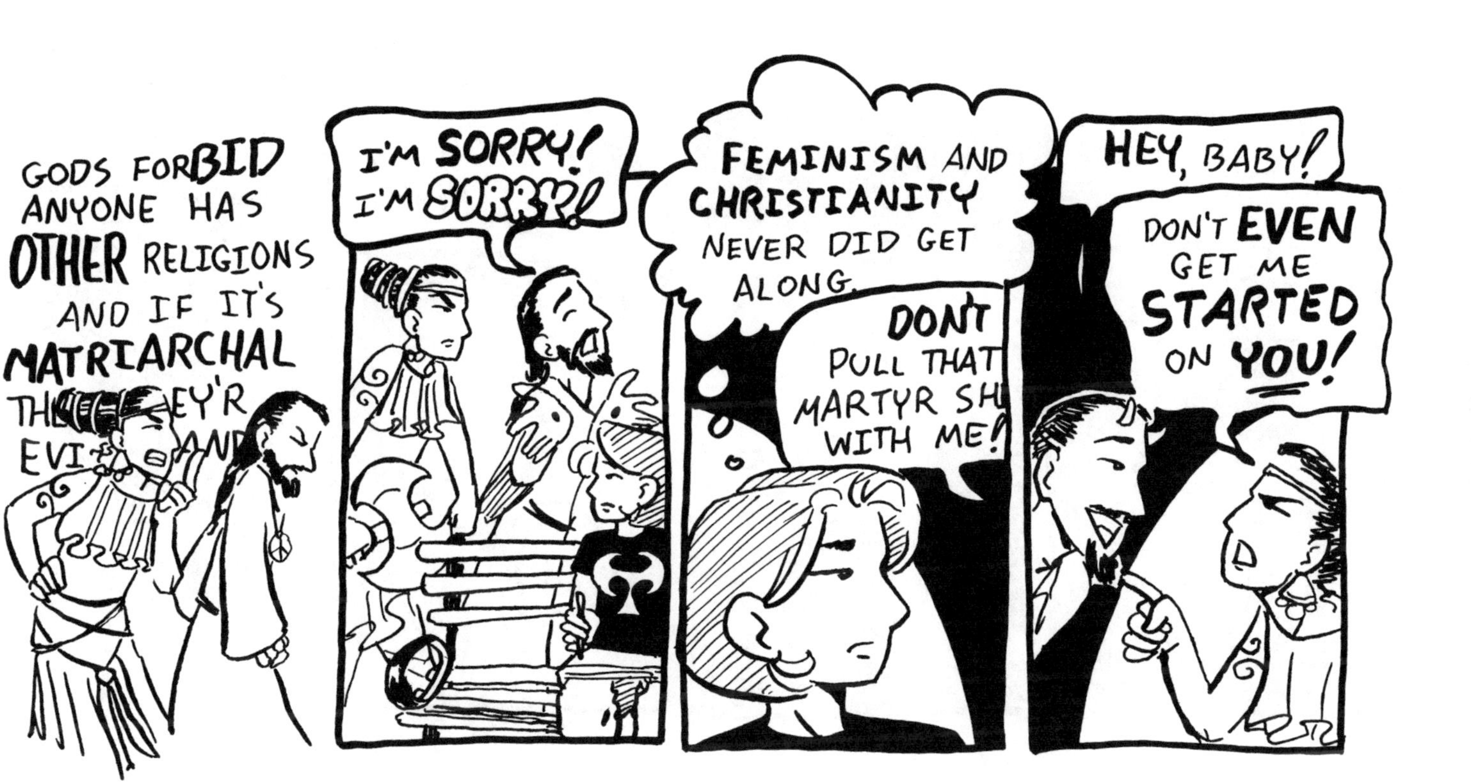
GODS FORBID ANYONE HAS OTHER RELIGIONS AND IF IT'S MATRIARCHAL
I'M SORRY! I'M SORRY!
FEMINISM AND CHRISTIANITY NEVER DID GET ALONG.
DON'T PULL THAT MARTYR SH WITH ME!
HEY, BABY!
DON'T EVEN GET ME STARTED ON YOU!

I SAID **NO** SUCH THING!!
DAMN EDITORS?

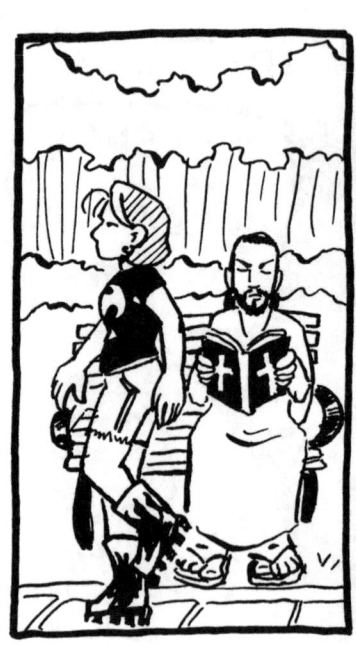

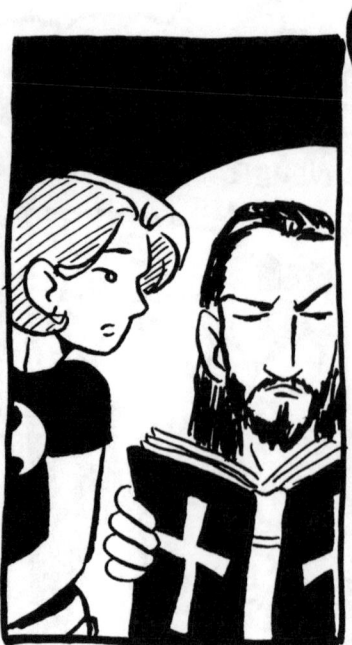

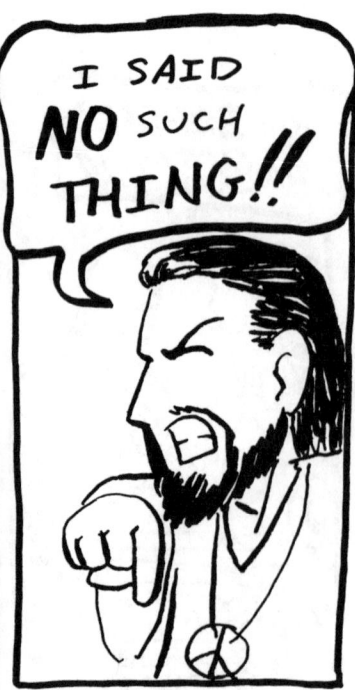

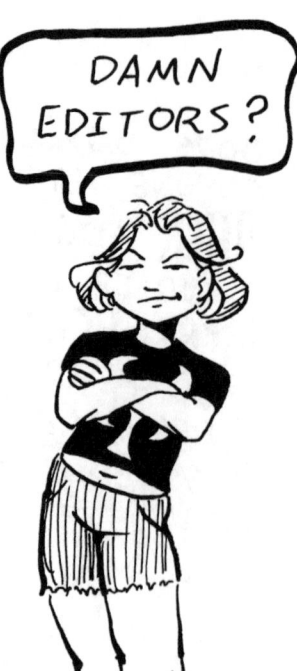

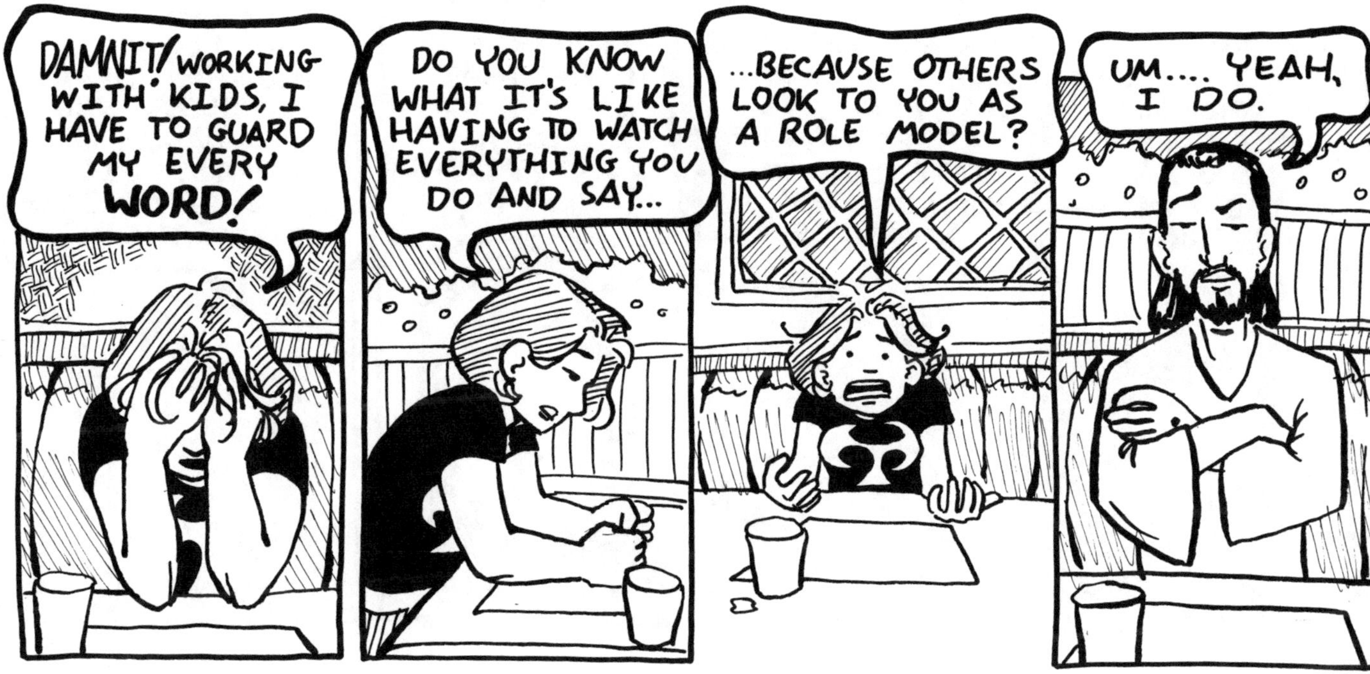
DAMNIT! WORKING WITH KIDS, I HAVE TO GUARD MY EVERY WORD!
DO YOU KNOW WHAT IT'S LIKE HAVING TO WATCH EVERYTHING YOU DO AND SAY...
...BECAUSE OTHERS LOOK TO YOU AS A ROLE MODEL?
UM.... YEAH, I DO.

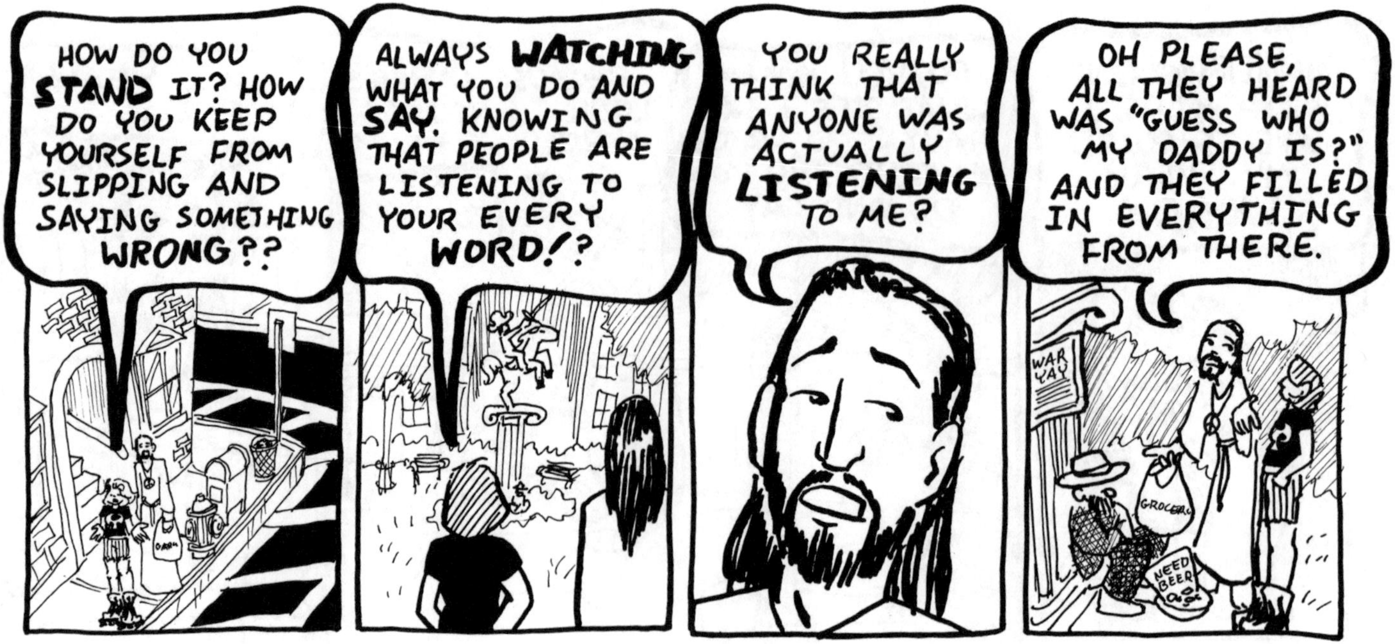
HOW DO YOU STAND IT? HOW DO YOU KEEP YOURSELF FROM SLIPPING AND SAYING SOMETHING WRONG??
ALWAYS WATCHING WHAT YOU DO AND SAY. KNOWING THAT PEOPLE ARE LISTENING TO YOUR EVERY WORD!?
YOU REALLY THINK THAT ANYONE WAS ACTUALLY LISTENING TO ME?
OH PLEASE, ALL THEY HEARD WAS "GUESS WHO MY DADDY IS?" AND THEY FILLED IN EVERYTHING FROM THERE.
WAR YAY
GROCERY
NEED BEER

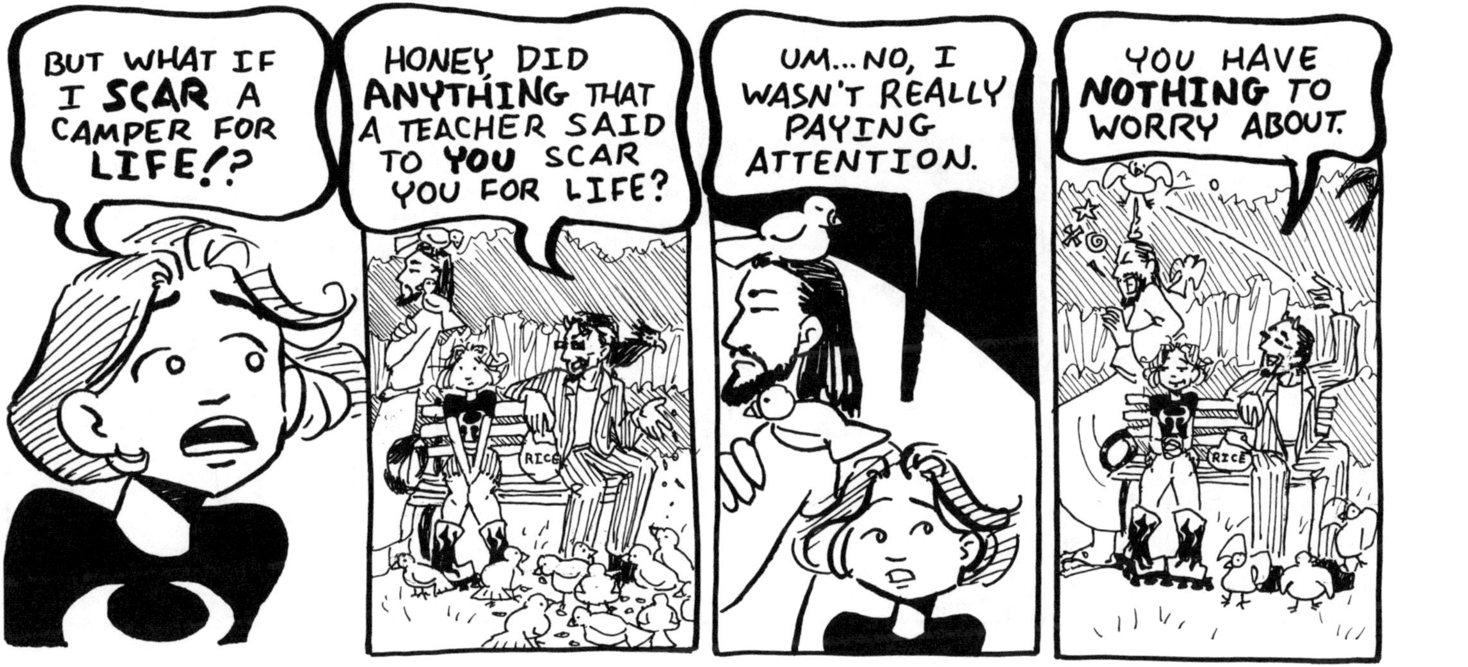
BUT WHAT IF I SCAR A CAMPER FOR LIFE!?
HONEY, DID ANYTHING THAT A TEACHER SAID TO YOU SCAR YOU FOR LIFE?
RICE
UM...NO, I WASN'T REALLY PAYING ATTENTION.
YOU HAVE NOTHING TO WORRY ABOUT.
RICE

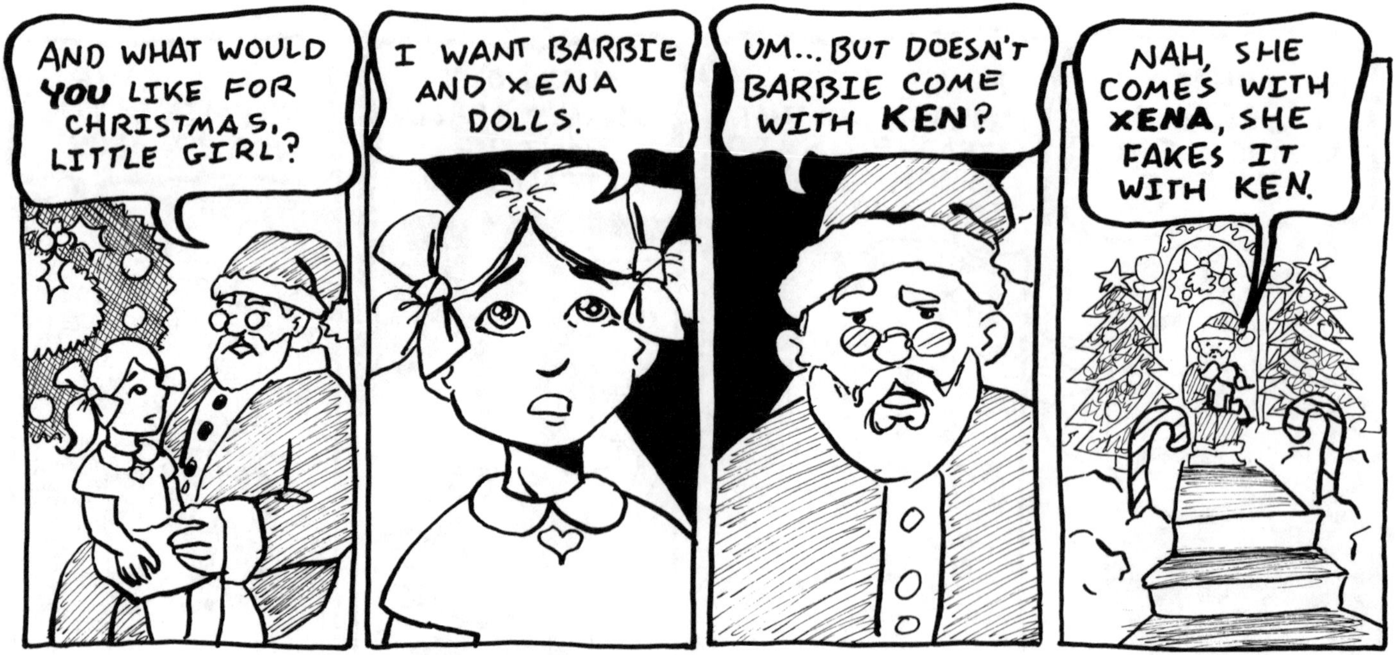
AND WHAT WOULD YOU LIKE FOR CHRISTMAS, LITTLE GIRL?
I WANT BARBIE AND XENA DOLLS.
UM... BUT DOESN'T BARBIE COME WITH KEN?
NAH, SHE COMES WITH XENA, SHE FAKES IT WITH KEN.

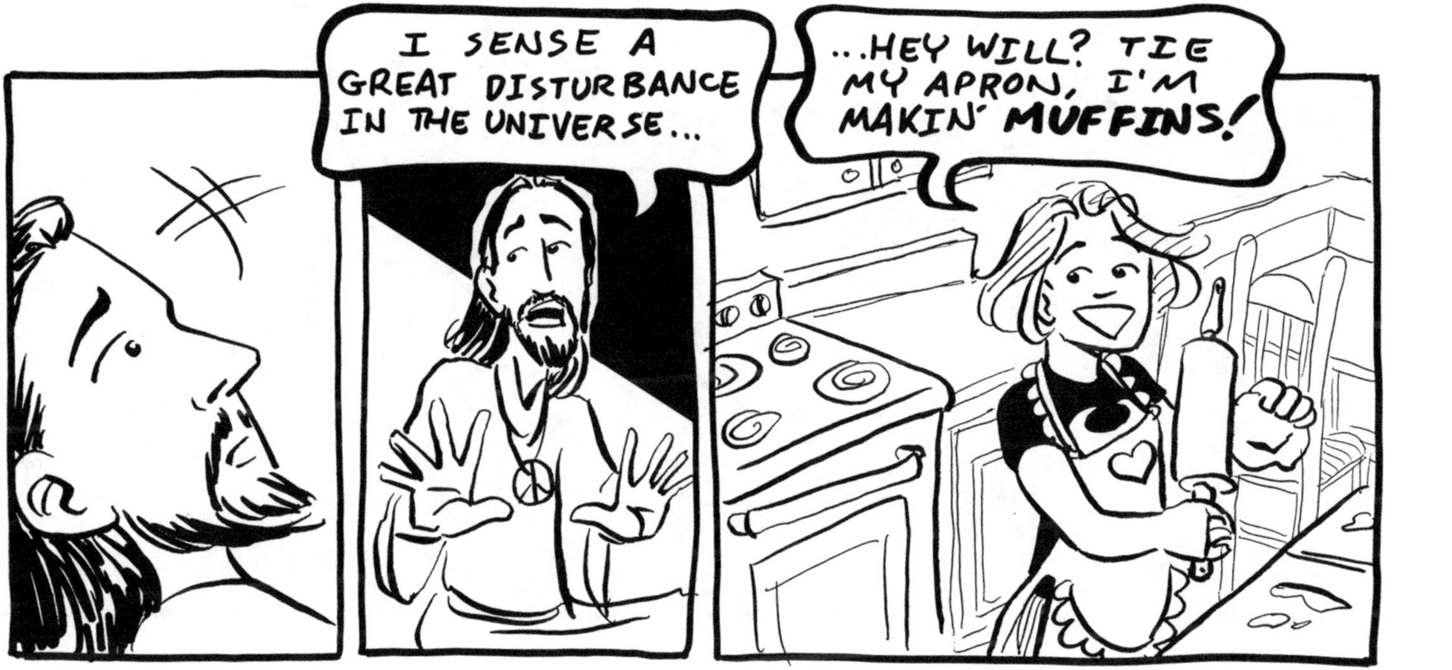
I SENSE A GREAT DISTURBANCE IN THE UNIVERSE...
...HEY WILL? TIE MY APRON, I'M MAKIN' MUFFINS!

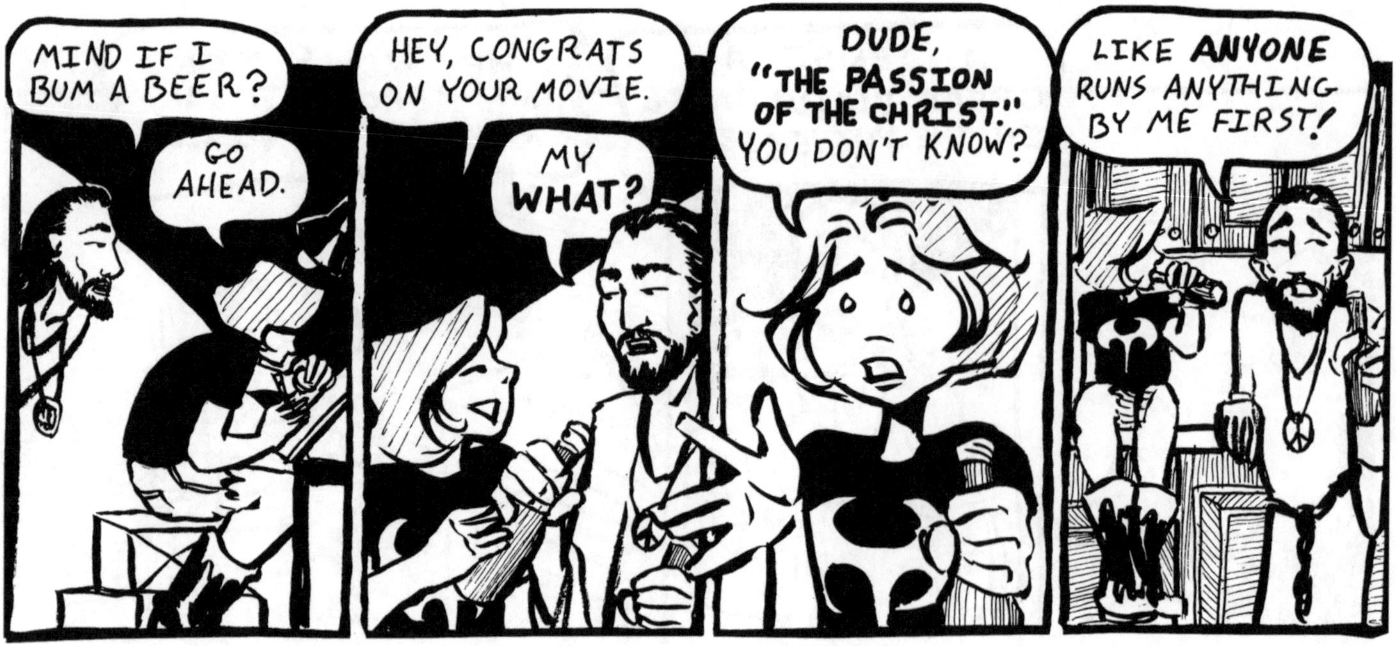

MIND IF I BUM A BEER?
GO AHEAD.
HEY, CONGRATS ON YOUR MOVIE.
MY **WHAT?**
DUDE, **"THE PASSION OF THE CHRIST."** YOU DON'T KNOW?
LIKE **ANYONE** RUNS ANYTHING BY ME FIRST!

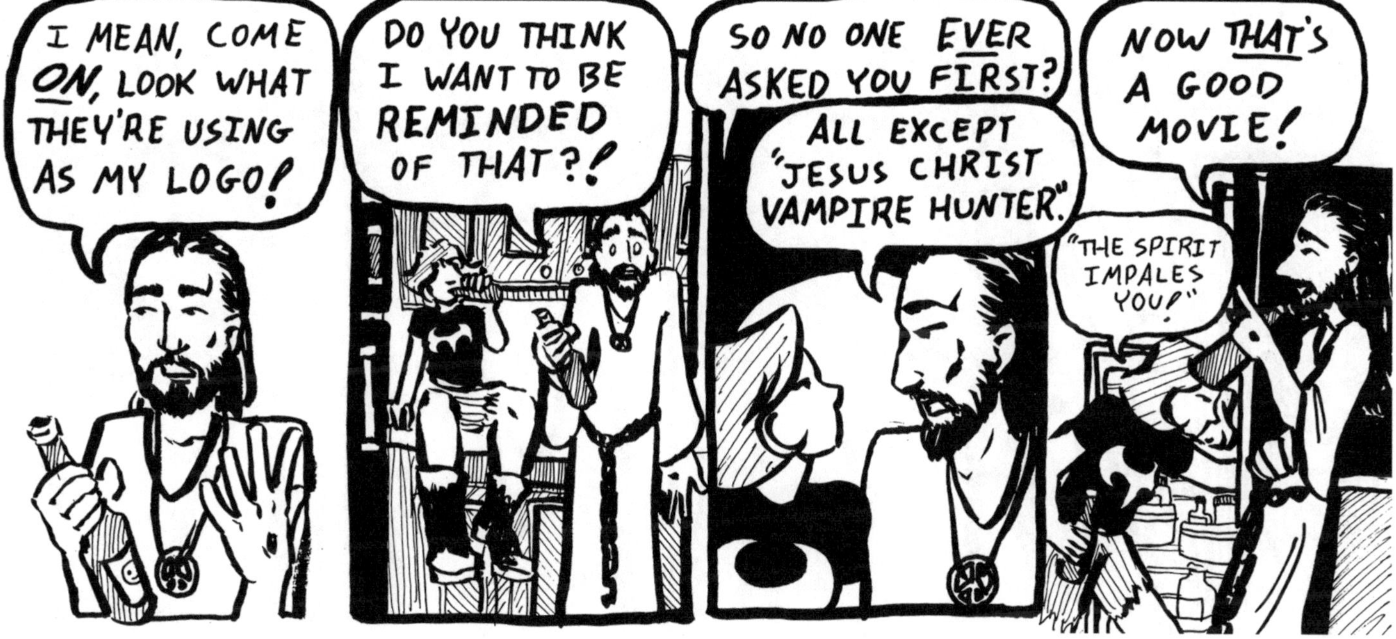
I MEAN, COME ON, LOOK WHAT THEY'RE USING AS MY LOGO!
DO YOU THINK I WANT TO BE REMINDED OF THAT?!
SO NO ONE EVER ASKED YOU FIRST?
ALL EXCEPT "JESUS CHRIST VAMPIRE HUNTER".
NOW THAT'S A GOOD MOVIE!
"THE SPIRIT IMPALES YOU!"

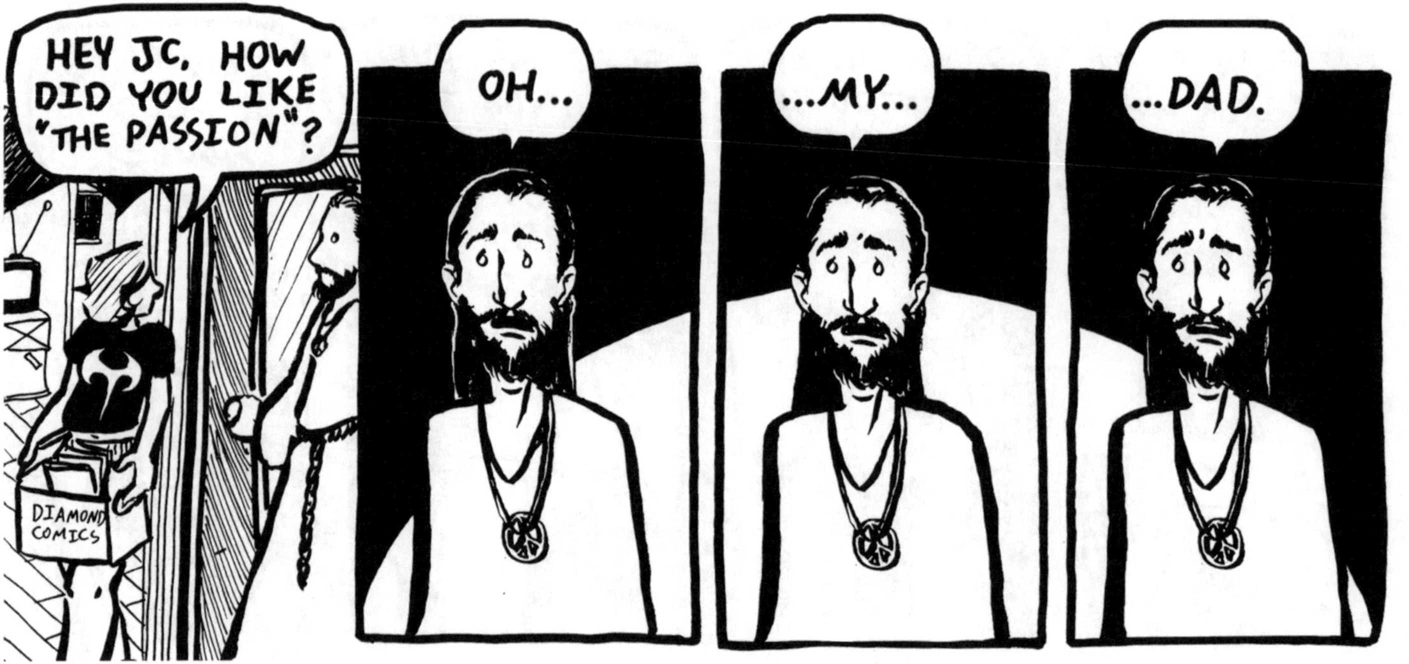
HEY JC, HOW DID YOU LIKE "THE PASSION"?
DIAMOND COMICS
OH...
...MY...
...DAD.

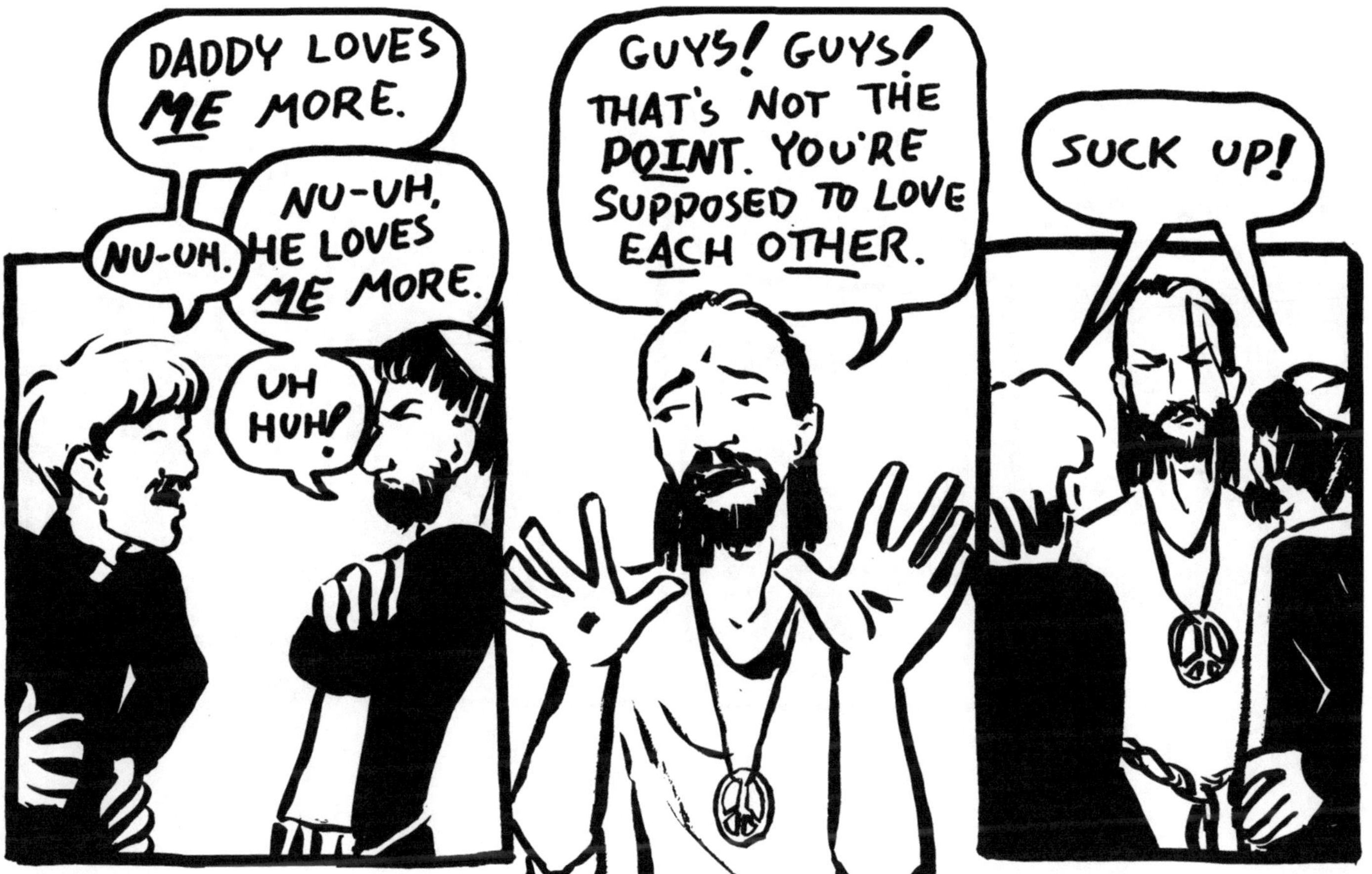
DADDY LOVES ME MORE.
NU-UH.
NU-UH, HE LOVES ME MORE.
UH HUH!
GUYS! GUYS! THAT'S NOT THE POINT. YOU'RE SUPPOSED TO LOVE EACH OTHER.
SUCK UP!

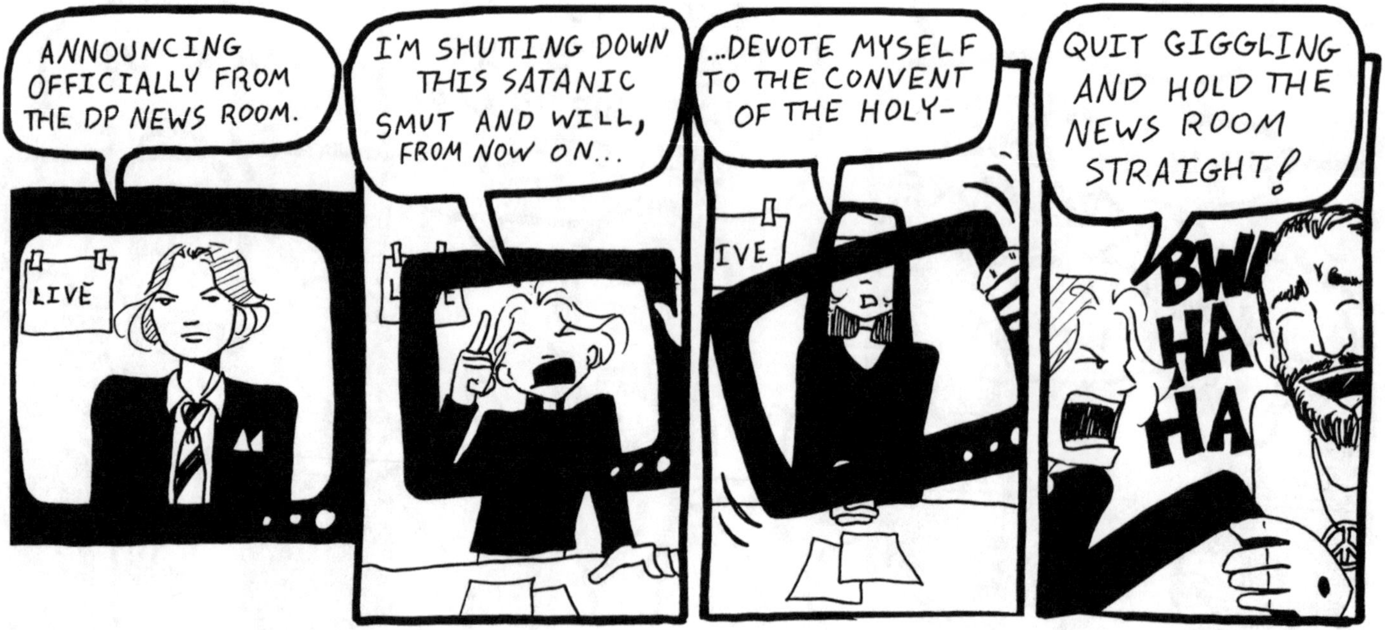
ANNOUNCING OFFICIALLY FROM THE DP NEWS ROOM.
LIVE
I'M SHUTTING DOWN THIS SATANIC SMUT AND WILL, FROM NOW ON...
...DEVOTE MYSELF TO THE CONVENT OF THE HOLY-
IVE
QUIT GIGGLING AND HOLD THE NEWS ROOM STRAIGHT!
BW HA HA HA

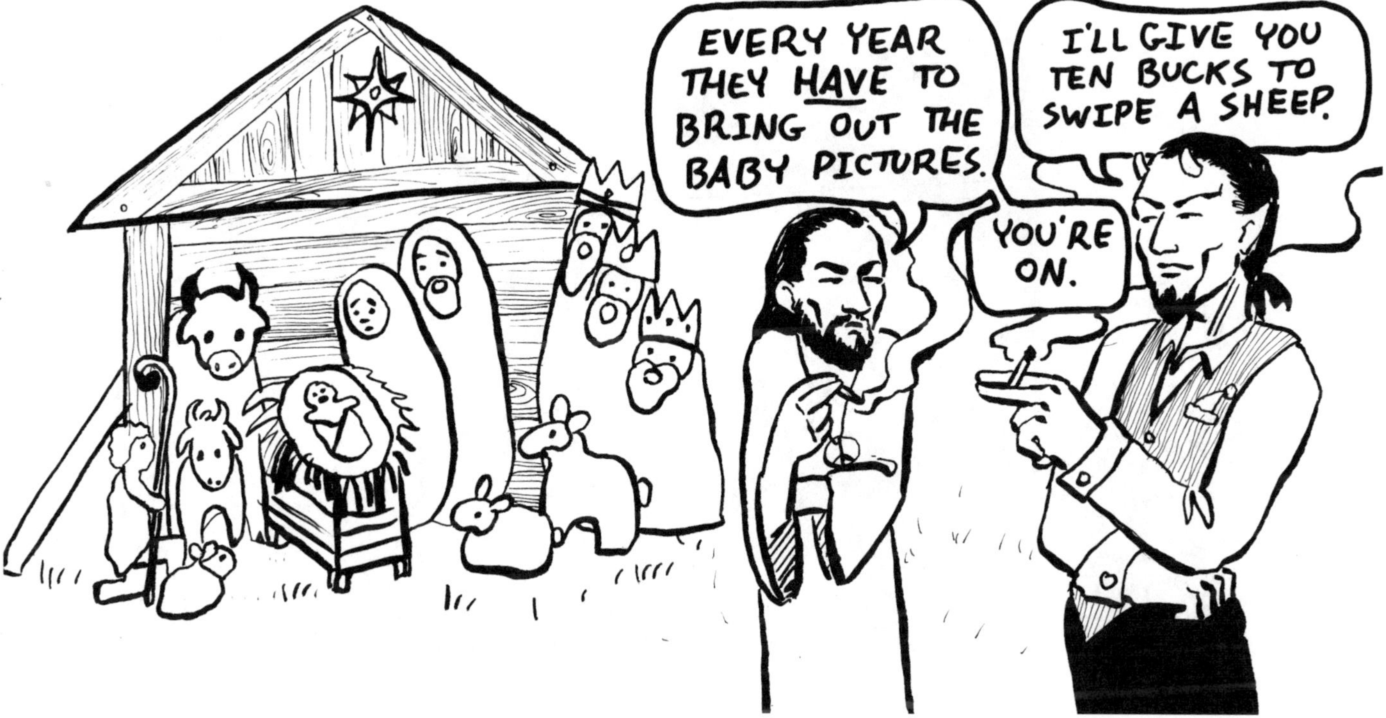
EVERY YEAR THEY HAVE TO BRING OUT THE BABY PICTURES.
I'LL GIVE YOU TEN BUCKS TO SWIPE A SHEEP.
YOU'RE ON.

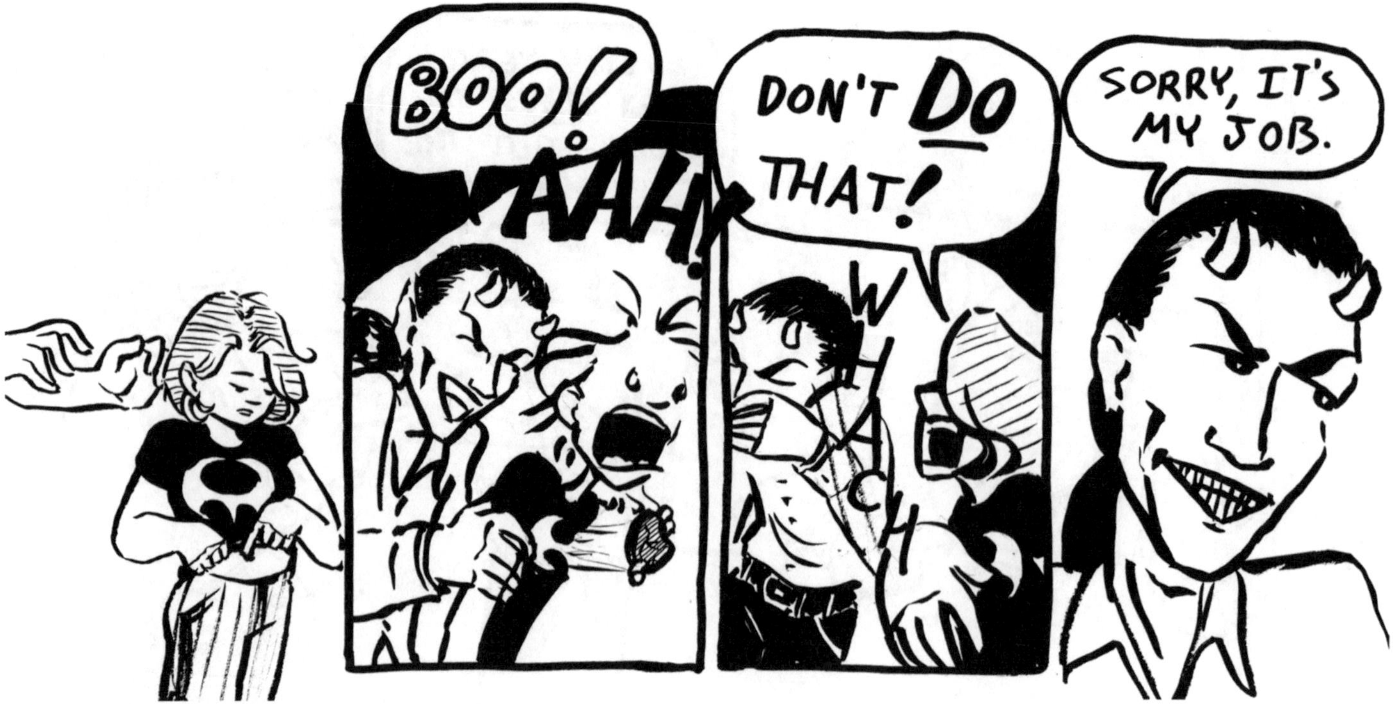
BOO!
AAAH!
DON'T DO THAT!
WHACH
SORRY, IT'S MY JOB.

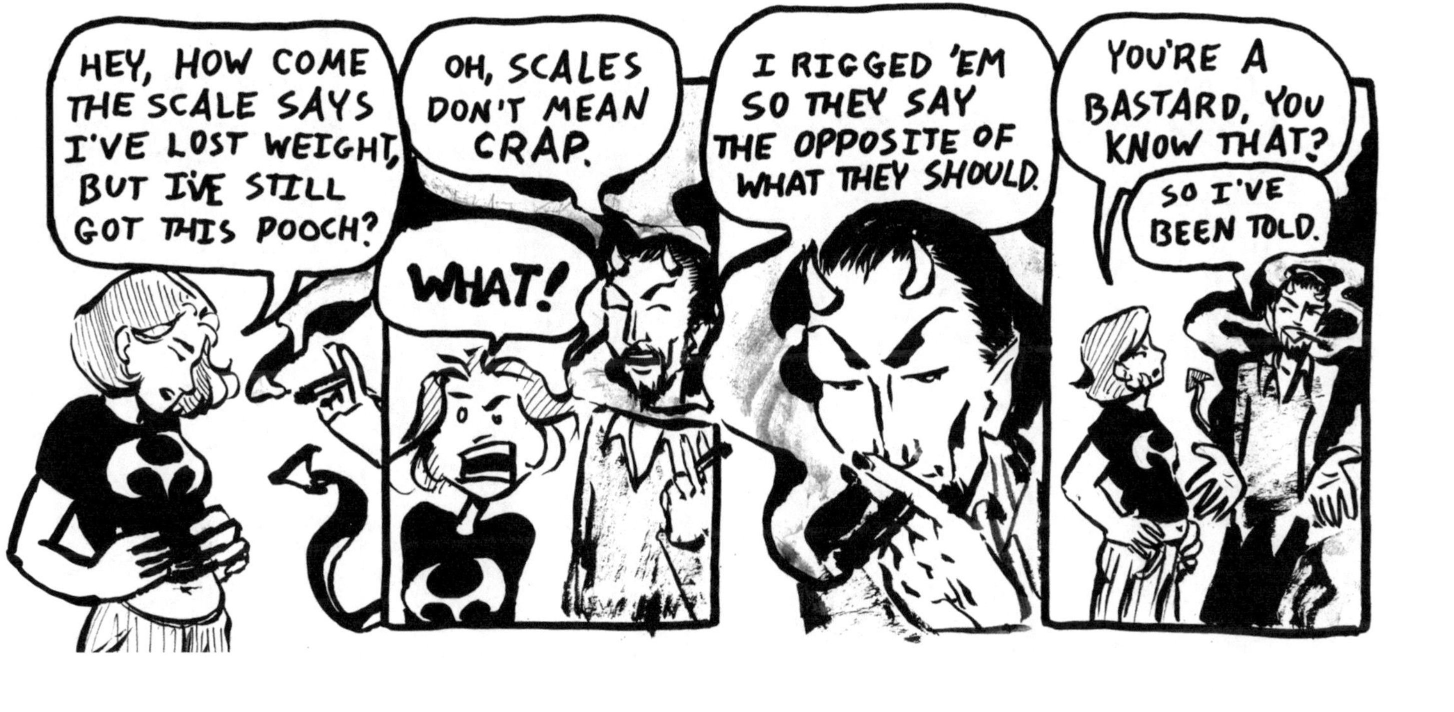
HEY, HOW COME THE SCALE SAYS I'VE LOST WEIGHT, BUT I'VE STILL GOT THIS POOCH?
OH, SCALES DON'T MEAN CRAP.
WHAT!
I RIGGED 'EM SO THEY SAY THE OPPOSITE OF WHAT THEY SHOULD.
YOU'RE A BASTARD, YOU KNOW THAT?
SO I'VE BEEN TOLD.

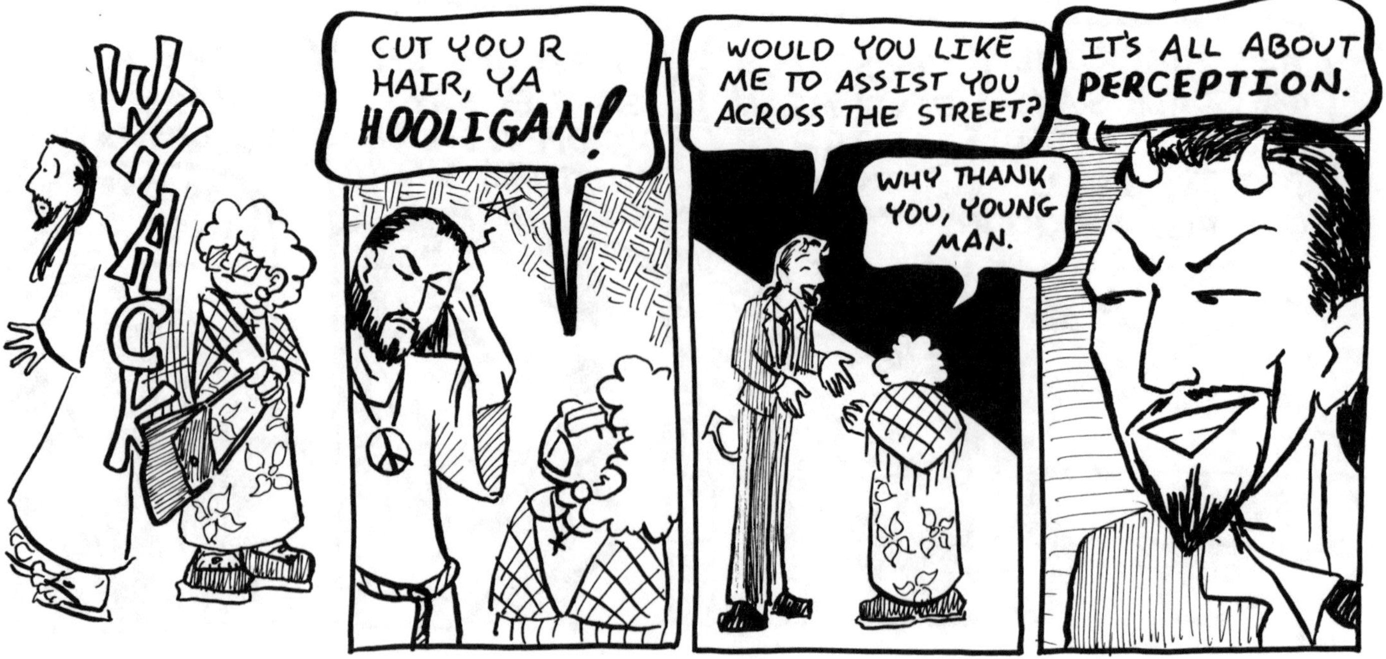
WHACK
CUT YOU R HAIR, YA HOOLIGAN!
WOULD YOU LIKE ME TO ASSIST YOU ACROSS THE STREET?
WHY THANK YOU, YOUNG MAN.
IT'S ALL ABOUT PERCEPTION.

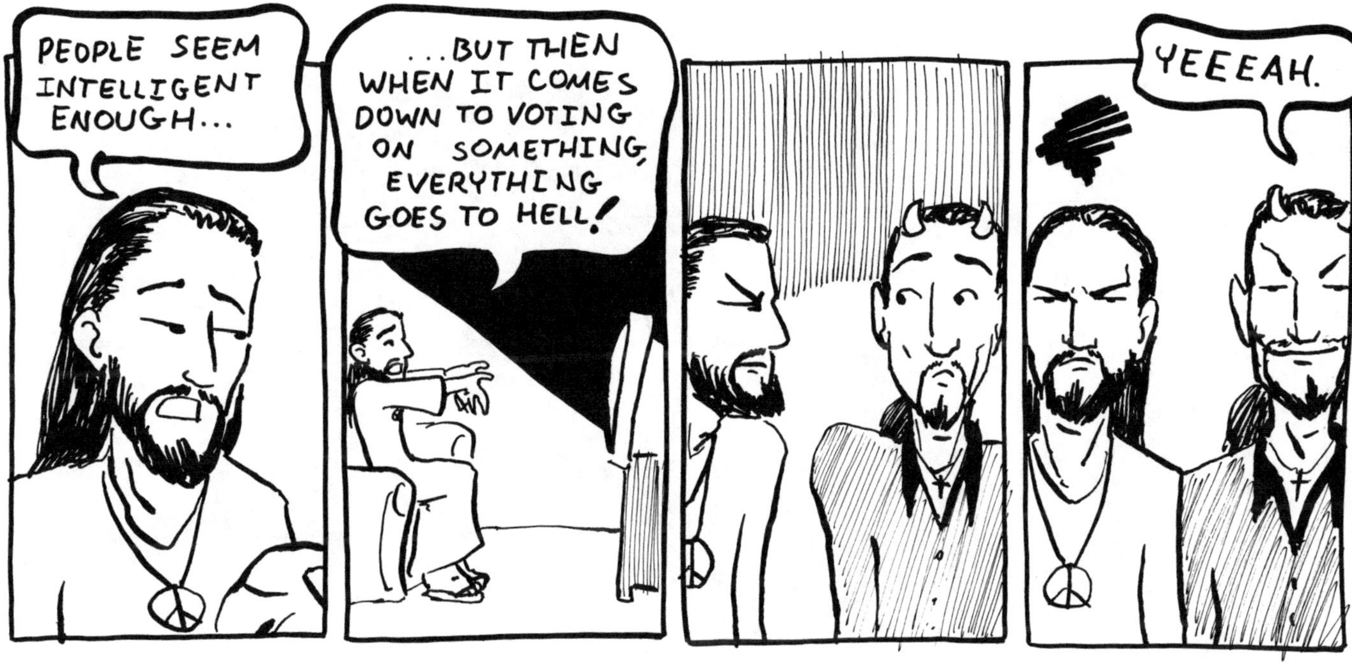
PEOPLE SEEM INTELLIGENT ENOUGH...
...BUT THEN WHEN IT COMES DOWN TO VOTING ON SOMETHING, EVERYTHING GOES TO HELL!
YEEEAH.

THAT WAS A GREAT CONVENTION.
I CAN'T BELIEVE WE WON THE COSTUME CONTEST.
WATCH OUT!
SCREECH!!
BAM!

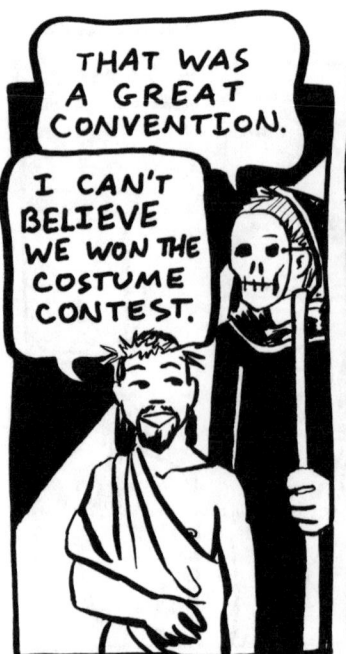

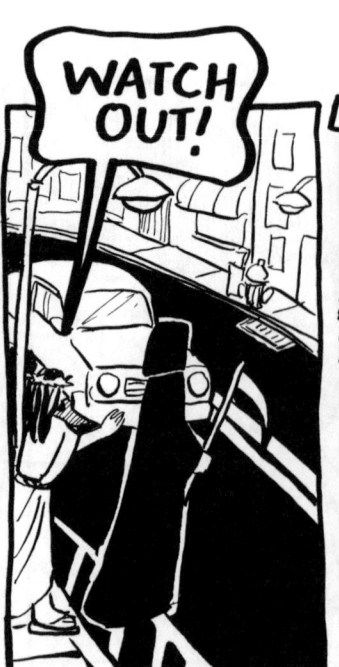

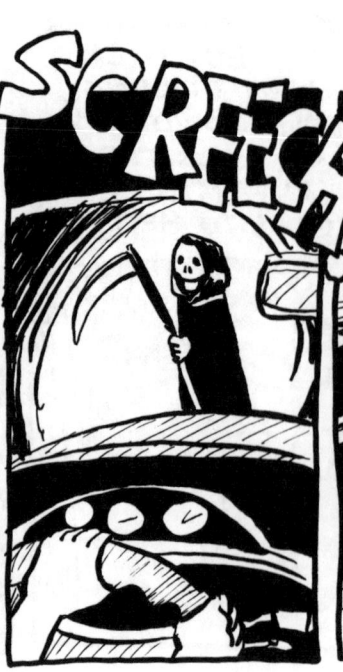

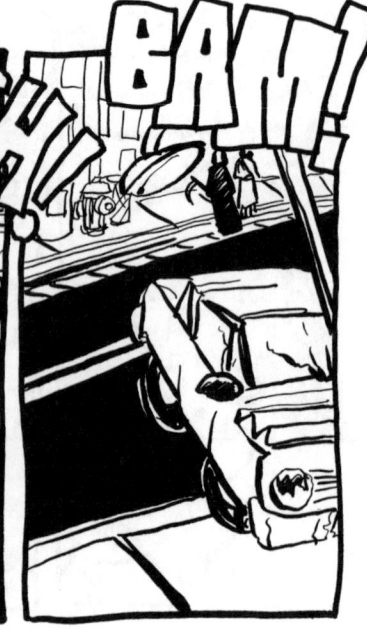

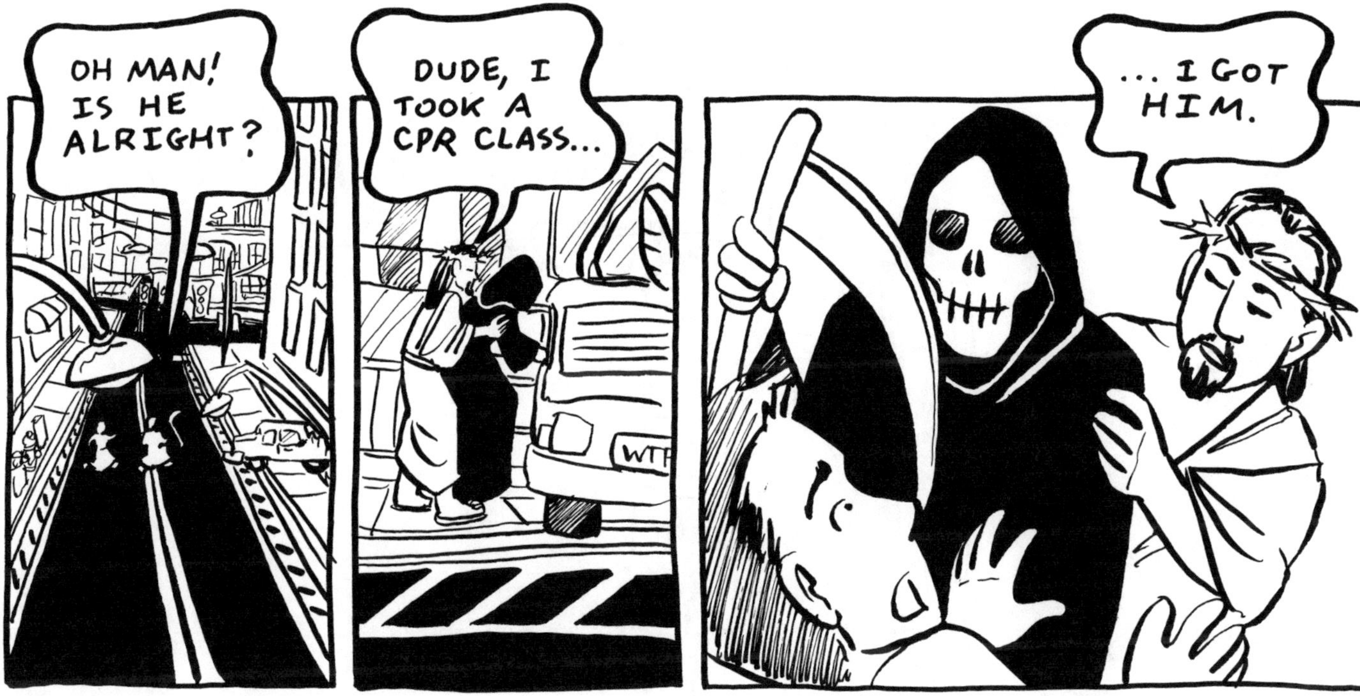

OH MAN! IS HE ALRIGHT?
DUDE, I TOOK A CPR CLASS...
WTF
... I GOT HIM.

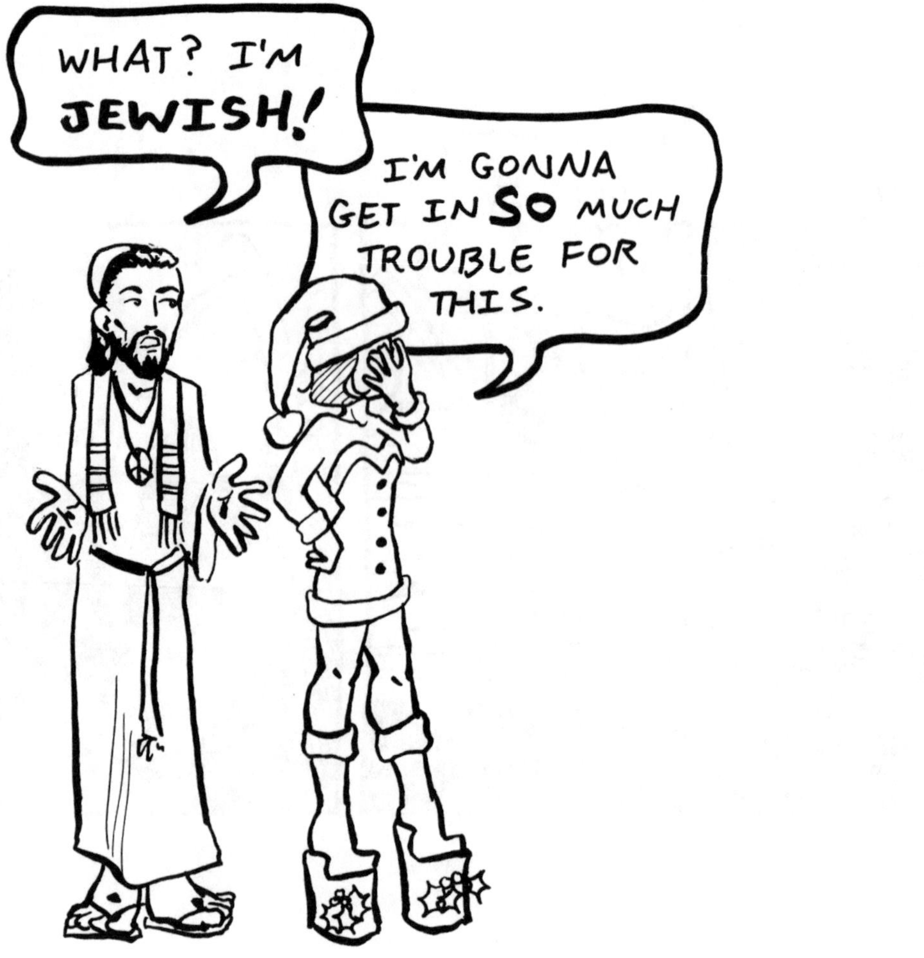
WHAT? I'M JEWISH!
I'M GONNA GET IN SO MUCH TROUBLE FOR THIS.

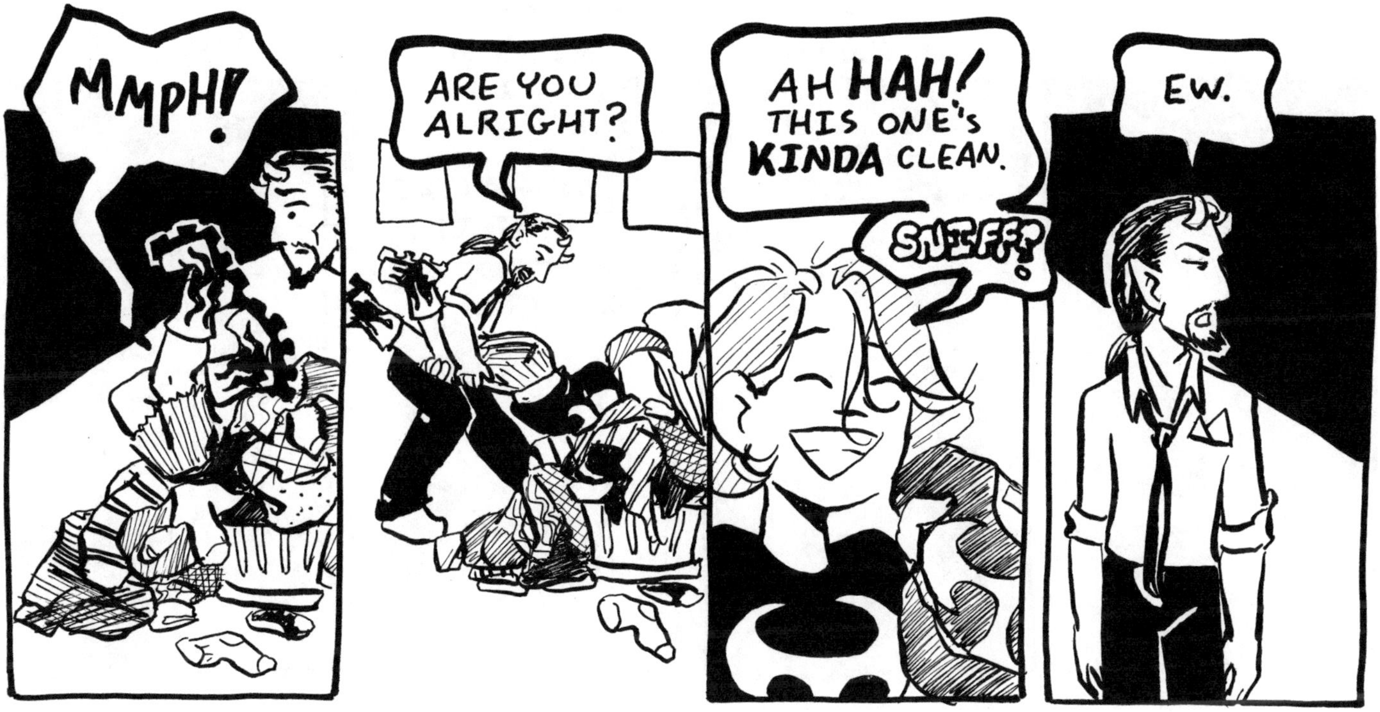
MMPH!
ARE YOU ALRIGHT?
AH HAH! THIS ONE'S KINDA CLEAN.
SNIFF!
EW.

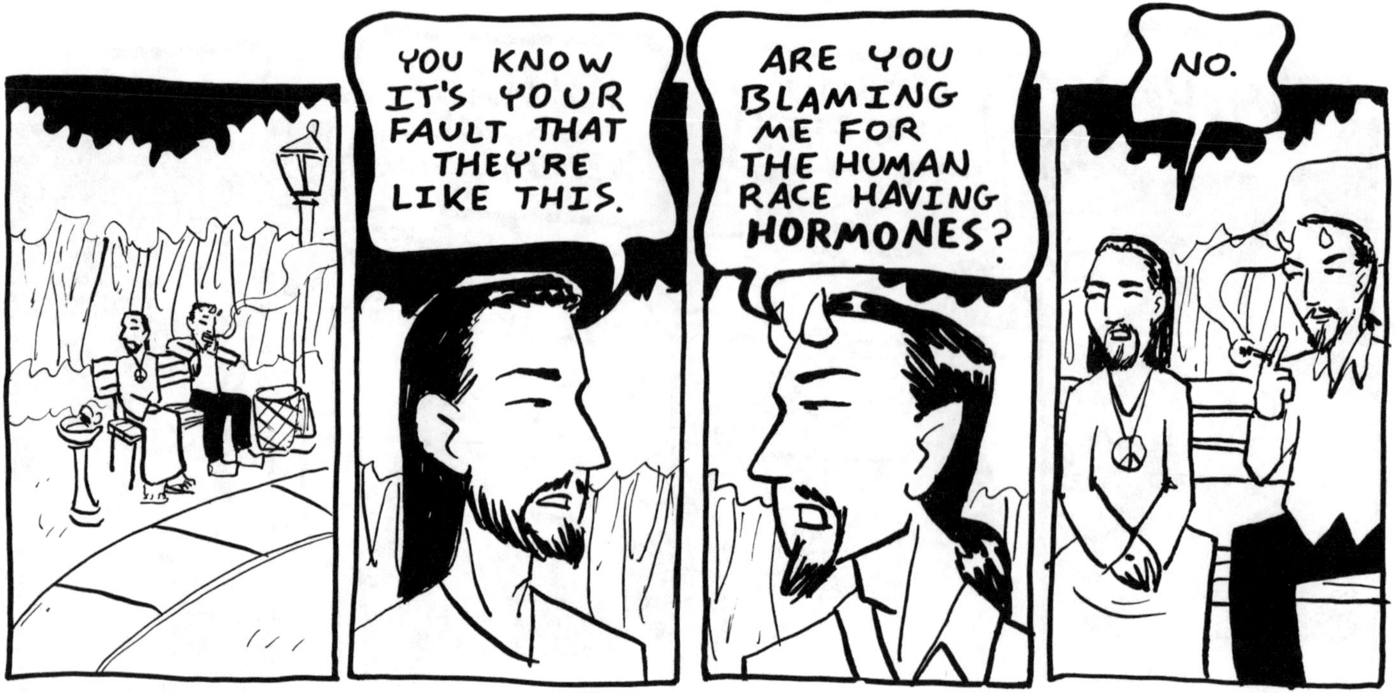
YOU KNOW IT'S YOUR FAULT THAT THEY'RE LIKE THIS.
ARE YOU BLAMING ME FOR THE HUMAN RACE HAVING HORMONES?
NO.

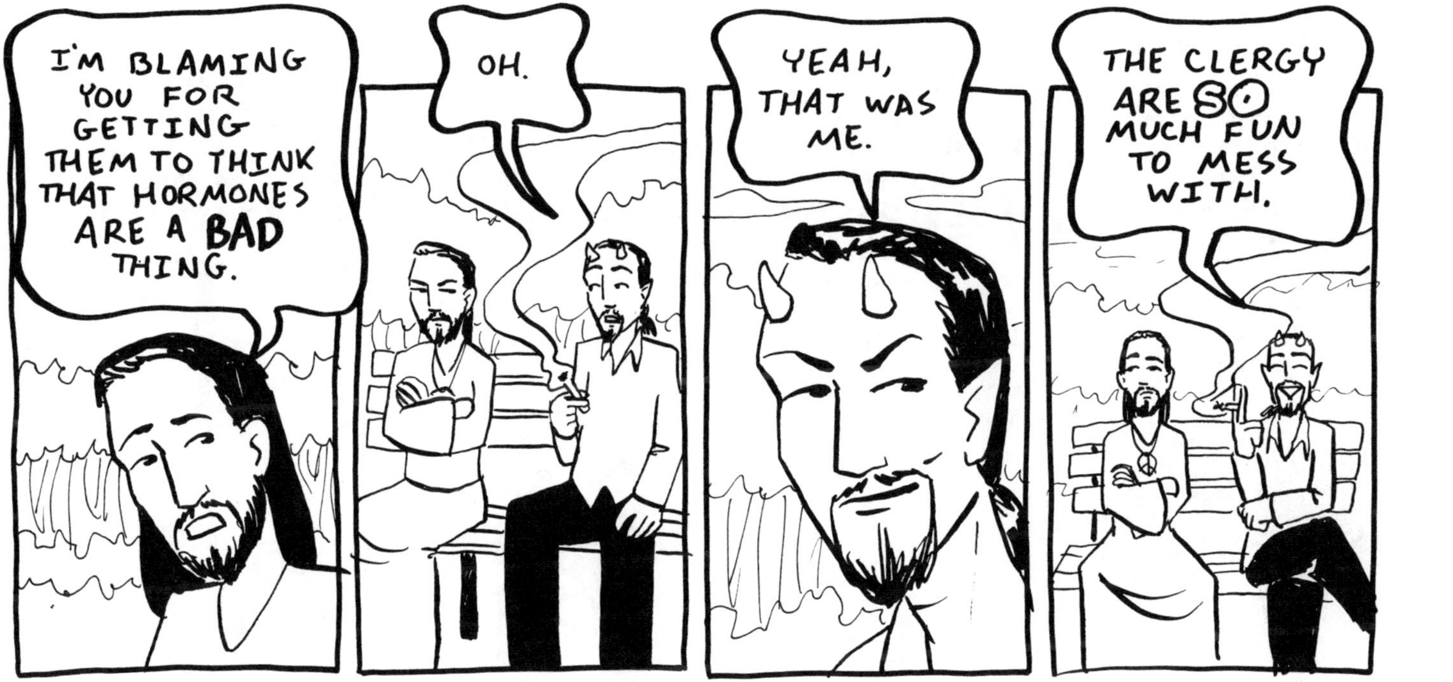
I'M BLAMING YOU FOR GETTING THEM TO THINK THAT HORMONES ARE A BAD THING.
OH.
YEAH, THAT WAS ME.
THE CLERGY ARE SO MUCH FUN TO MESS WITH.

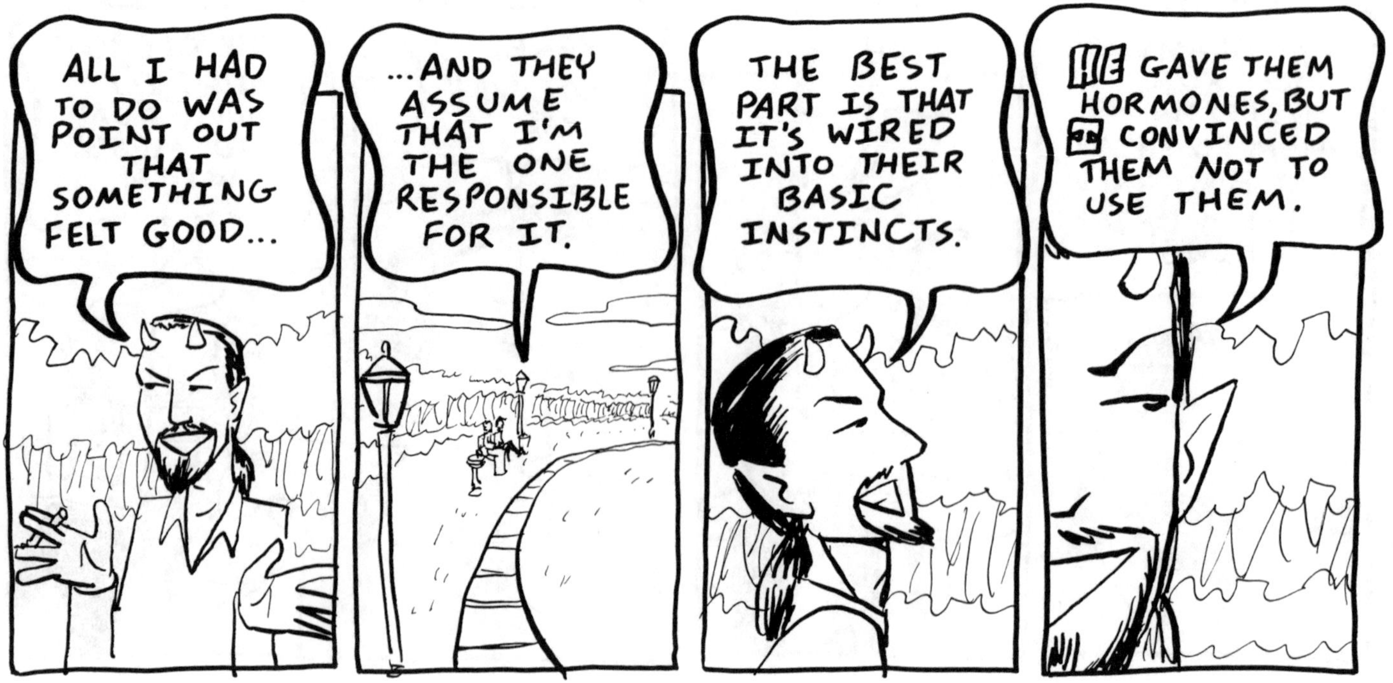
ALL I HAD TO DO WAS POINT OUT THAT SOMETHING FELT GOOD...
...AND THEY ASSUME THAT I'M THE ONE RESPONSIBLE FOR IT.
THE BEST PART IS THAT IT'S WIRED INTO THEIR BASIC INSTINCTS.
HE GAVE THEM HORMONES, BUT CONVINCED THEM NOT TO USE THEM.

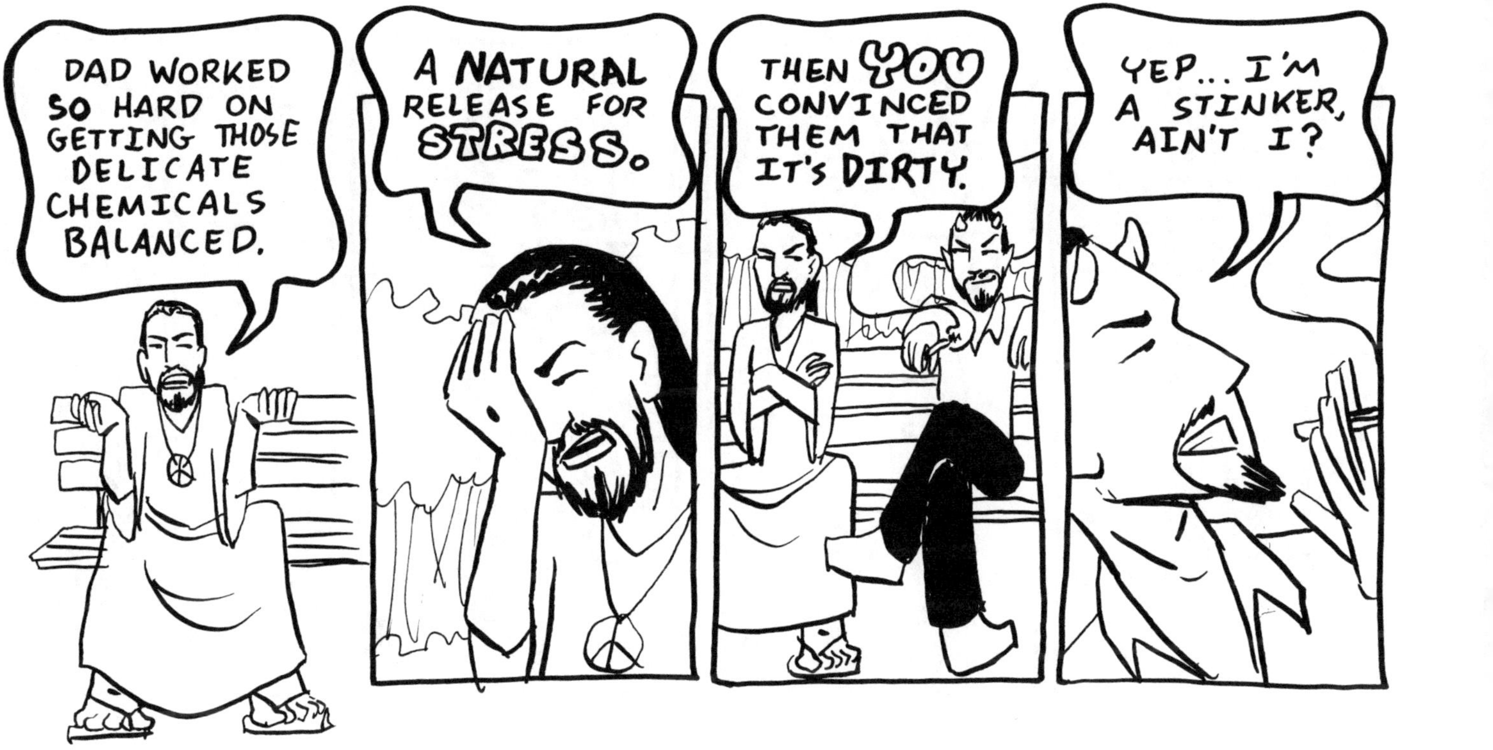
DAD WORKED SO HARD ON GETTING THOSE DELICATE CHEMICALS BALANCED.
A NATURAL RELEASE FOR STRESS.
THEN YOU CONVINCED THEM THAT IT'S DIRTY.
YEP... I'M A STINKER, AIN'T I?

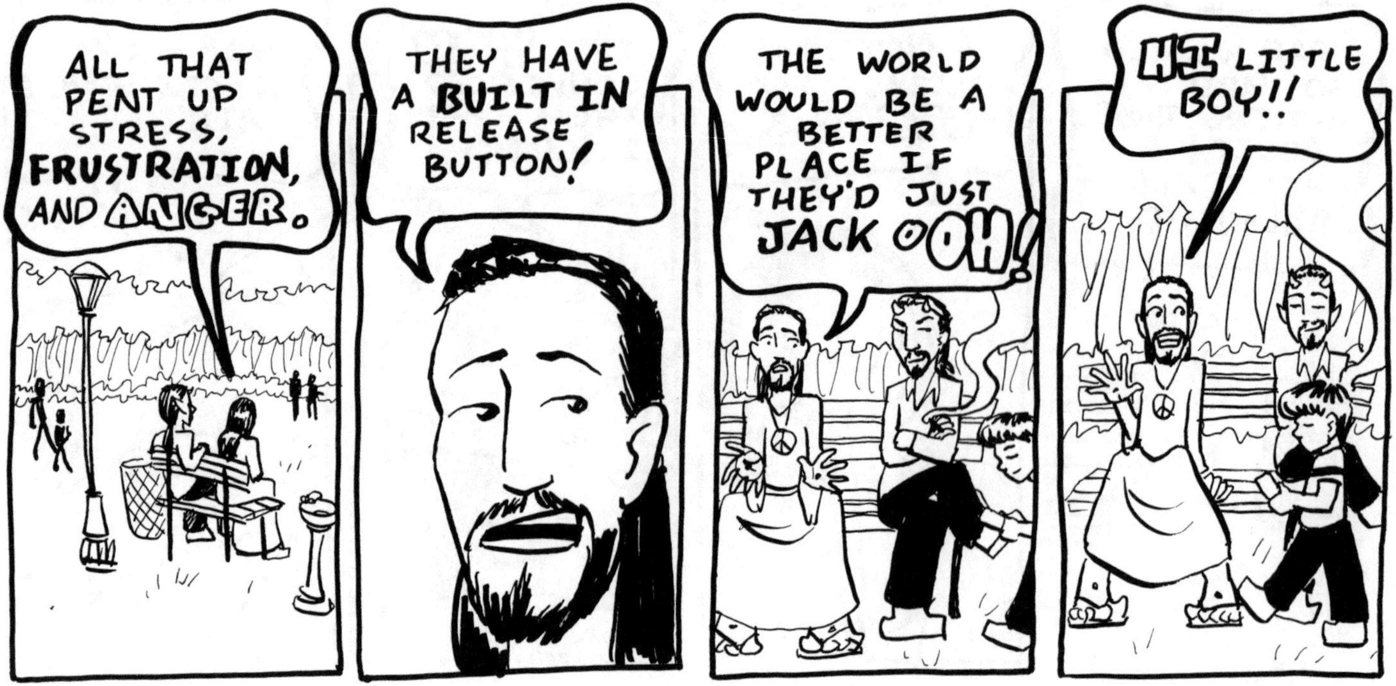
ALL THAT PENT UP STRESS, FRUSTRATION, AND ANGER.
THEY HAVE A BUILT IN RELEASE BUTTON!
THE WORLD WOULD BE A BETTER PLACE IF THEY'D JUST JACK OOH!
HI LITTLE BOY!!

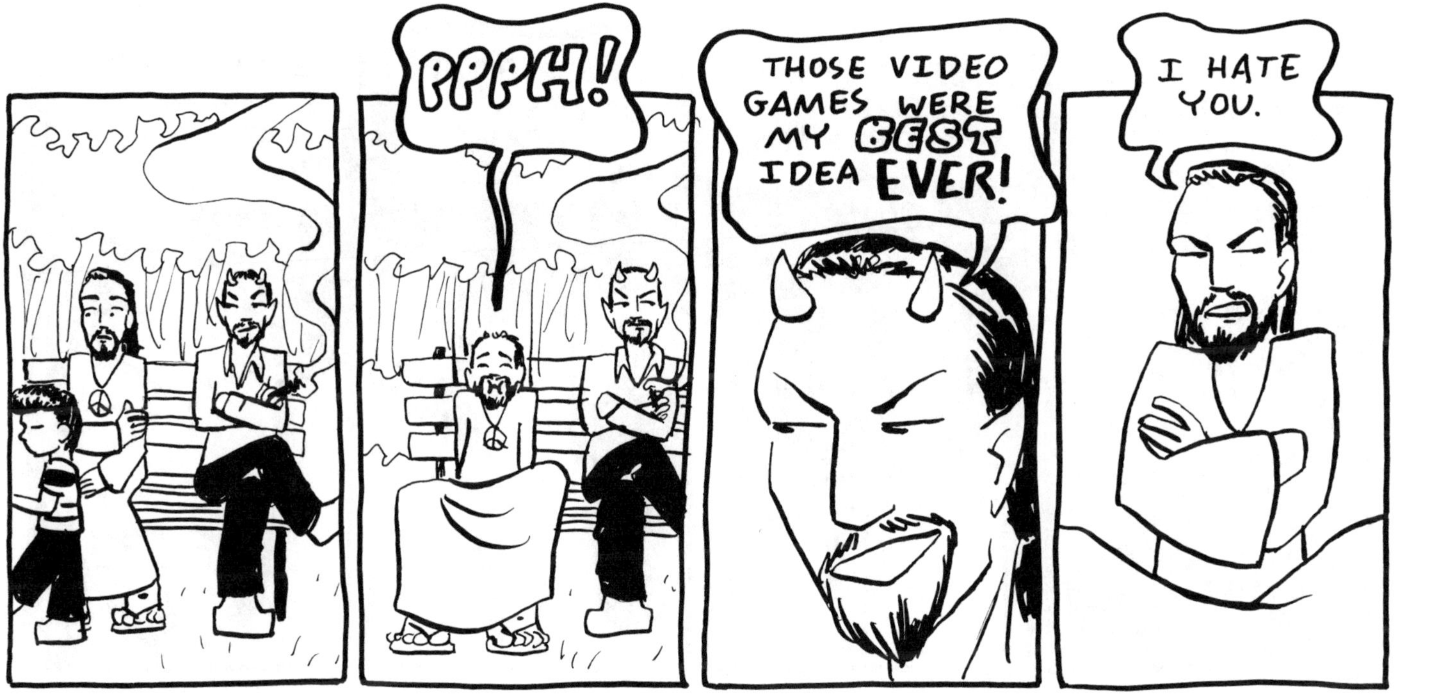
PPPH!
THOSE VIDEO GAMES WERE MY BEST IDEA EVER!
I HATE YOU.

THE OLYMPICS IS BROUGHT TO YOU BY COCA-COLA, BRINGING THE WORLD TOGETHER...
...AND McDONALDS, FEEDING THE ATHLETES...
...AND "BODY OF LIES". IN THEATERS NEAR YOU.
'S COOL HOW I WORKED THAT IN THERE, RIGHT?

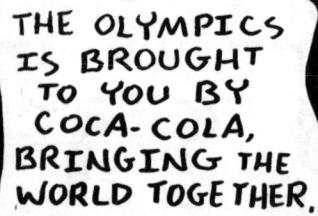

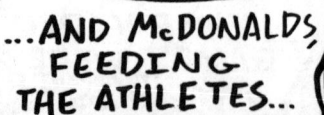

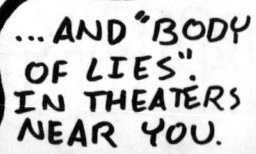

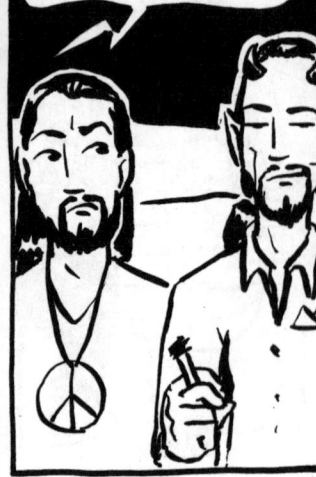

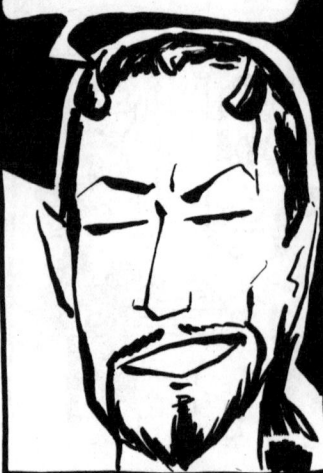

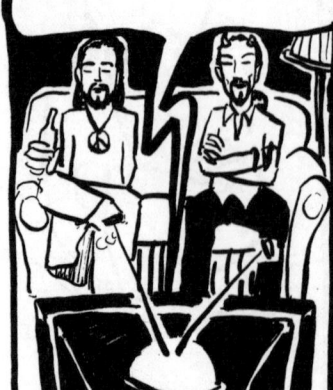

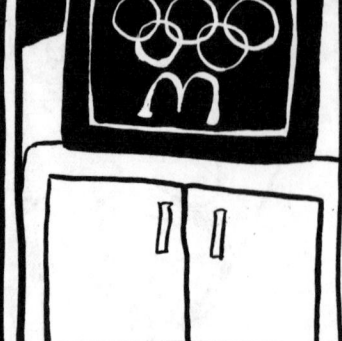

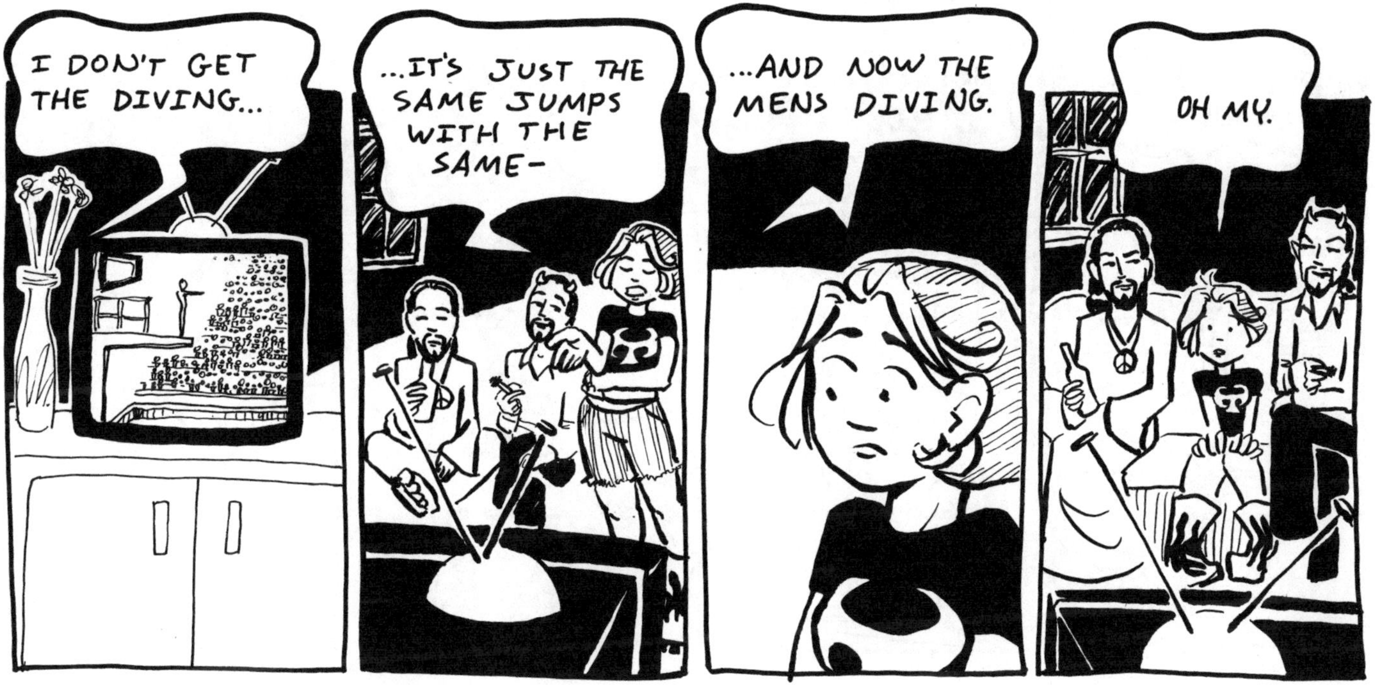
I DON'T GET THE DIVING...
...IT'S JUST THE SAME JUMPS WITH THE SAME-
...AND NOW THE MENS DIVING.
OH MY.

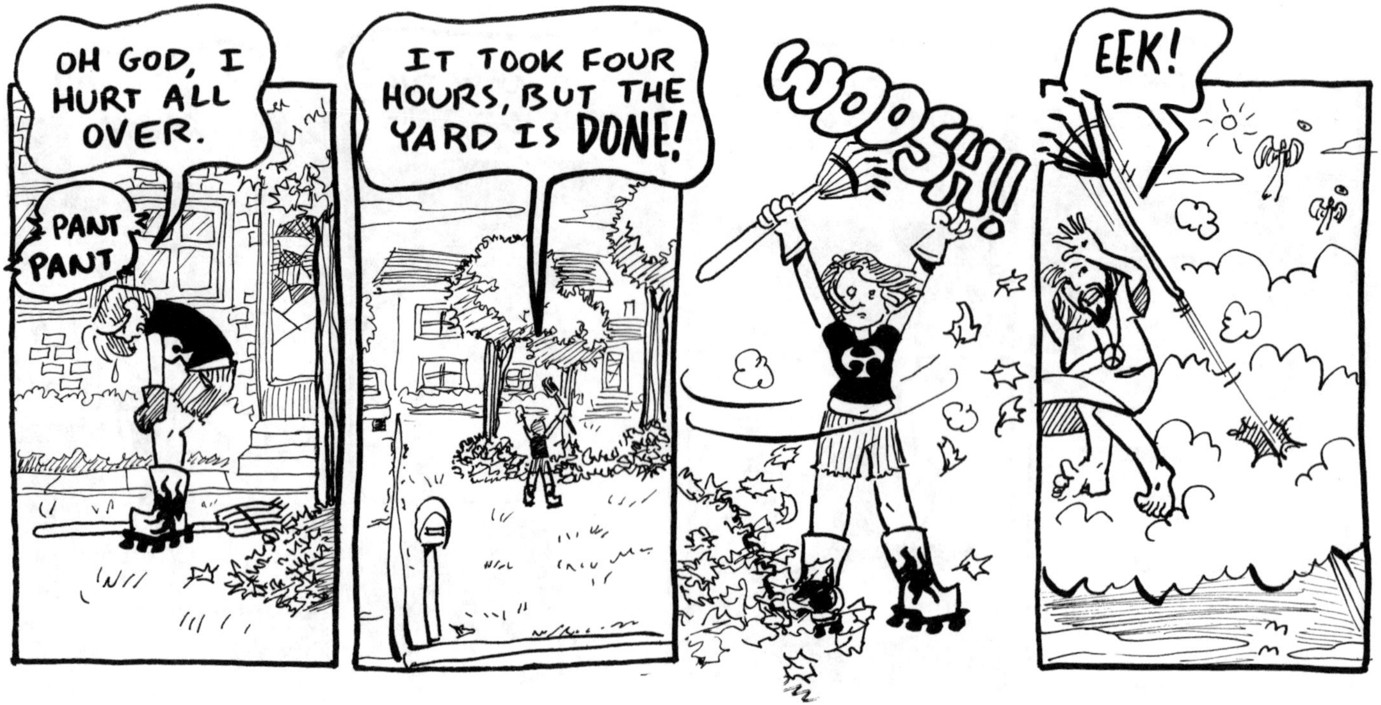
OH GOD, I HURT ALL OVER.
PANT PANT
IT TOOK FOUR HOURS, BUT THE YARD IS DONE!
WOOSH!
EEK!

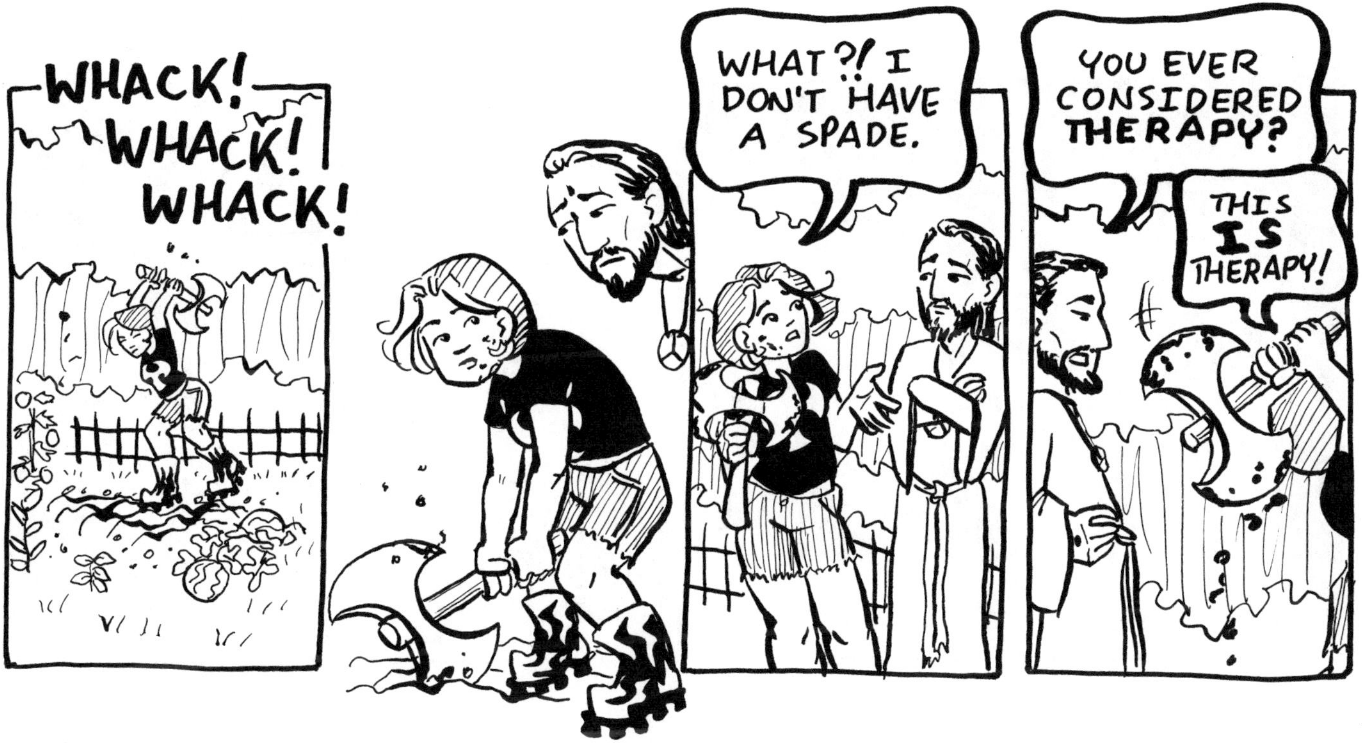
WHACK! WHACK! WHACK!
WHAT?! I DON'T HAVE A SPADE.
YOU EVER CONSIDERED THERAPY?
THIS IS THERAPY!

HEY JC, YOU WANT A BEER?
GOD YES!

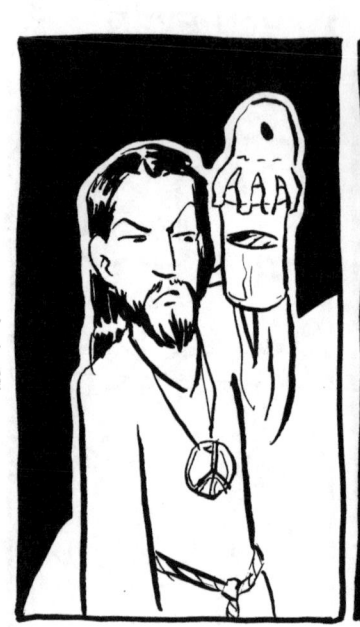

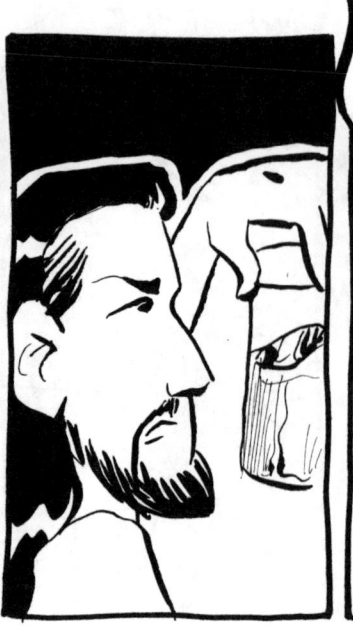

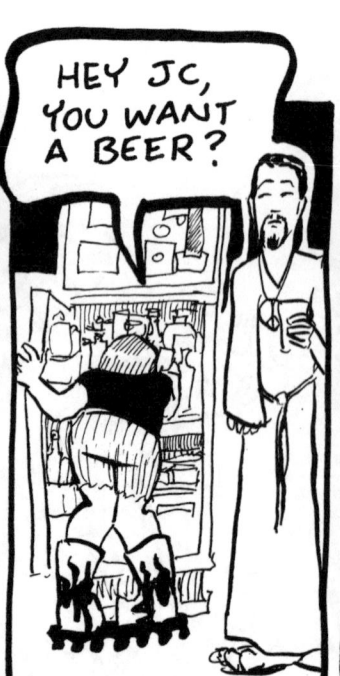

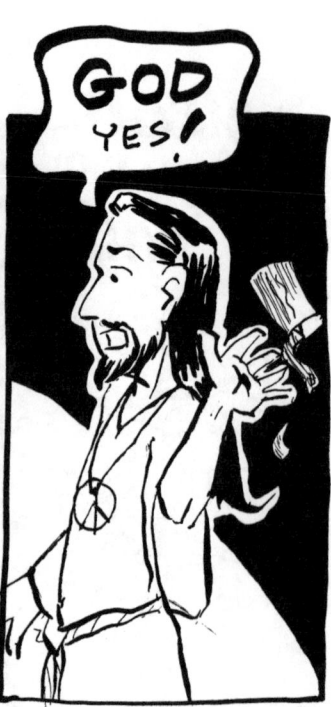

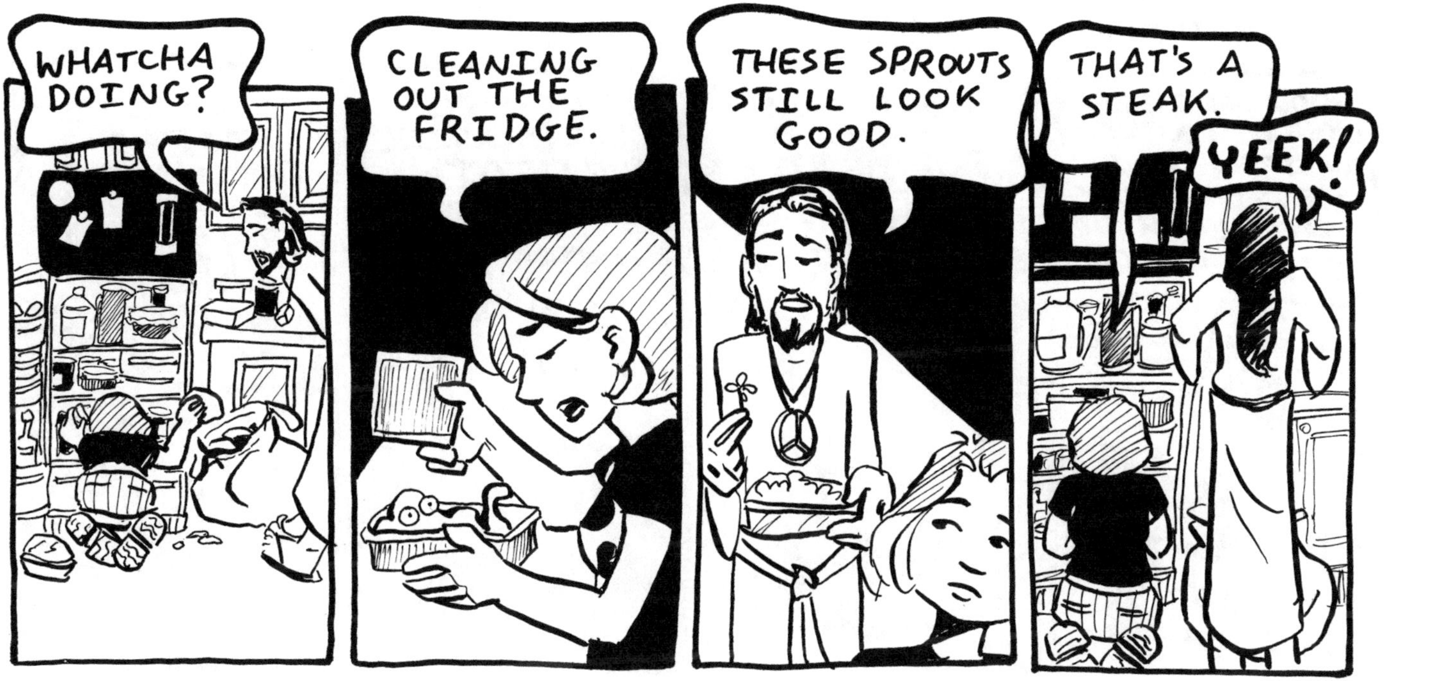
WHATCHA DOING?
CLEANING OUT THE FRIDGE.
THESE SPROUTS STILL LOOK GOOD.
THAT'S A STEAK.
YEEK!

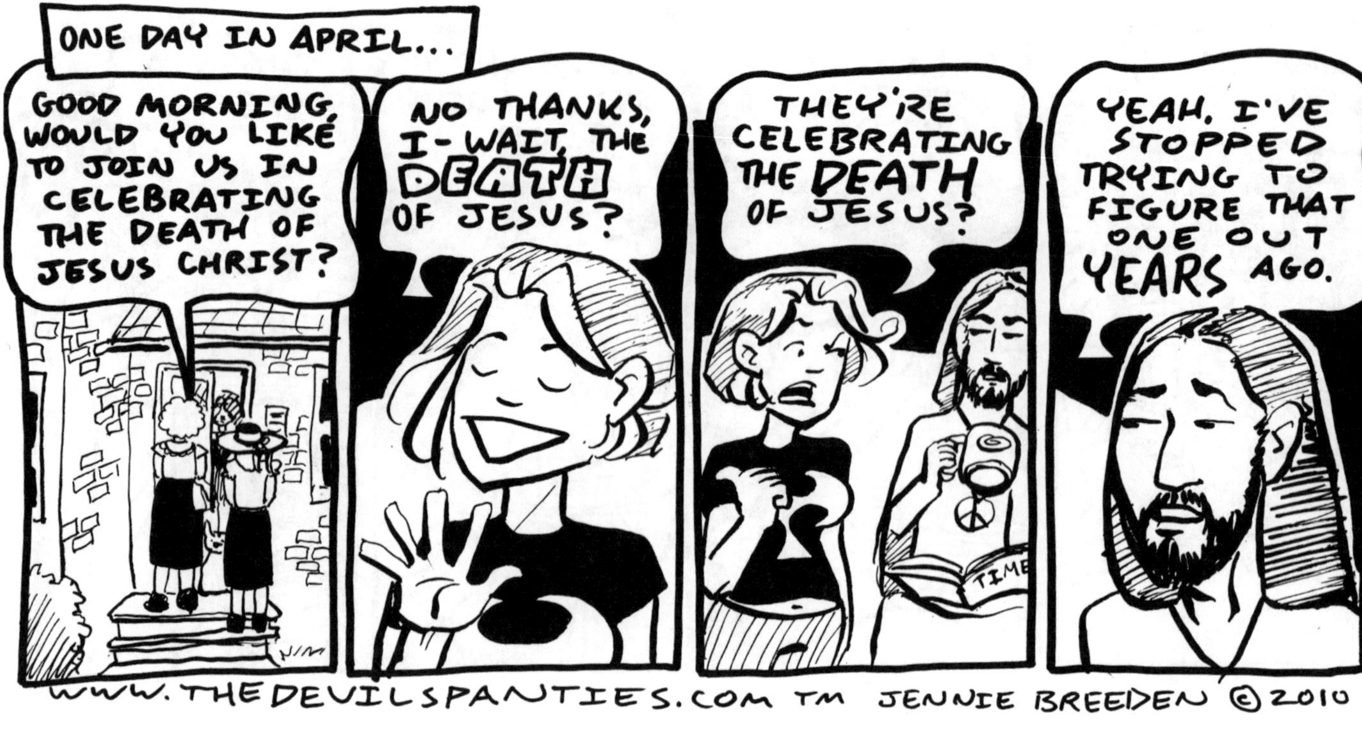
ONE DAY IN APRIL...
GOOD MORNING, WOULD YOU LIKE TO JOIN US IN CELEBRATING THE DEATH OF JESUS CHRIST?
NO THANKS, I- WAIT, THE DEATH OF JESUS?
THEY'RE CELEBRATING THE DEATH OF JESUS?
TIME
YEAH, I'VE STOPPED TRYING TO FIGURE THAT ONE OUT YEARS AGO.
WWW.THEDEVILSPANTIES.COM TM JENNIE BREEDEN ©2010

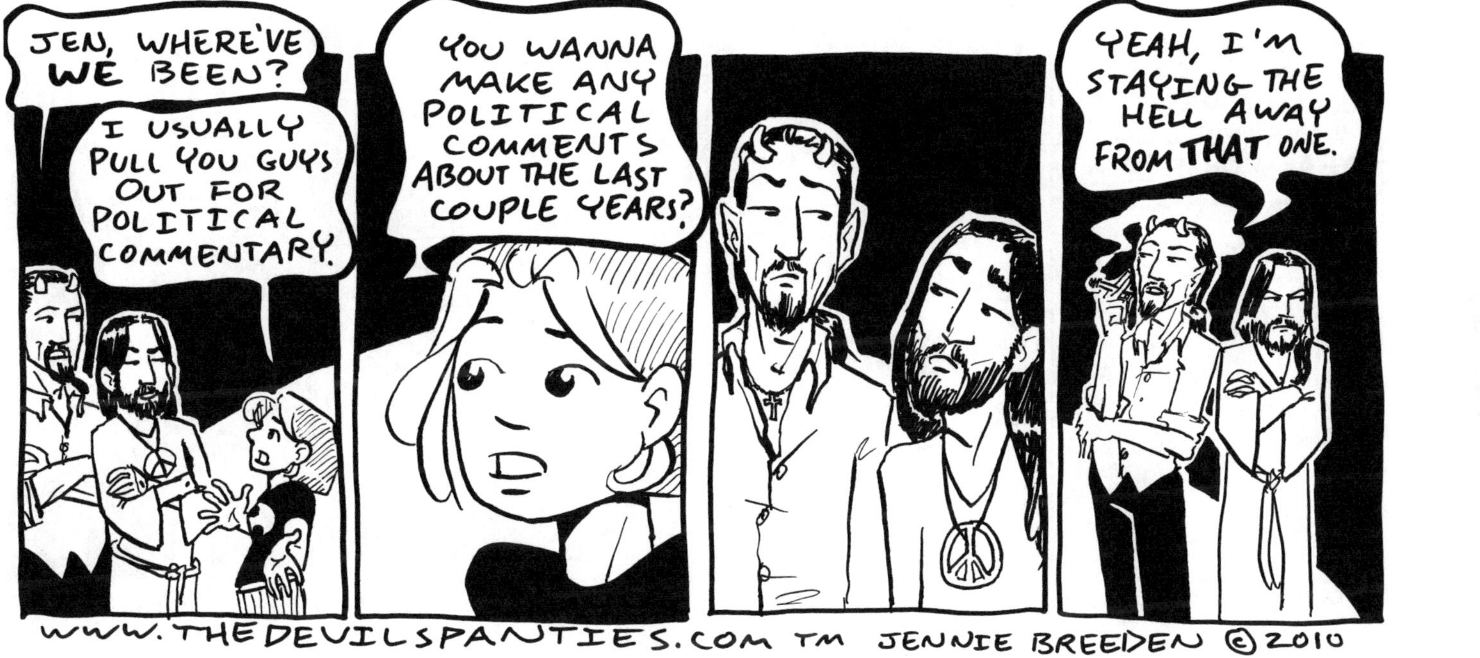
JEN, WHERE'VE WE BEEN?
I USUALLY PULL YOU GUYS OUT FOR POLITICAL COMMENTARY.
YOU WANNA MAKE ANY POLITICAL COMMENTS ABOUT THE LAST COUPLE YEARS?
YEAH, I'M STAYING THE HELL AWAY FROM THAT ONE.
WWW.THEDEVILSPANTIES.COM TM JENNIE BREEDEN ©2010

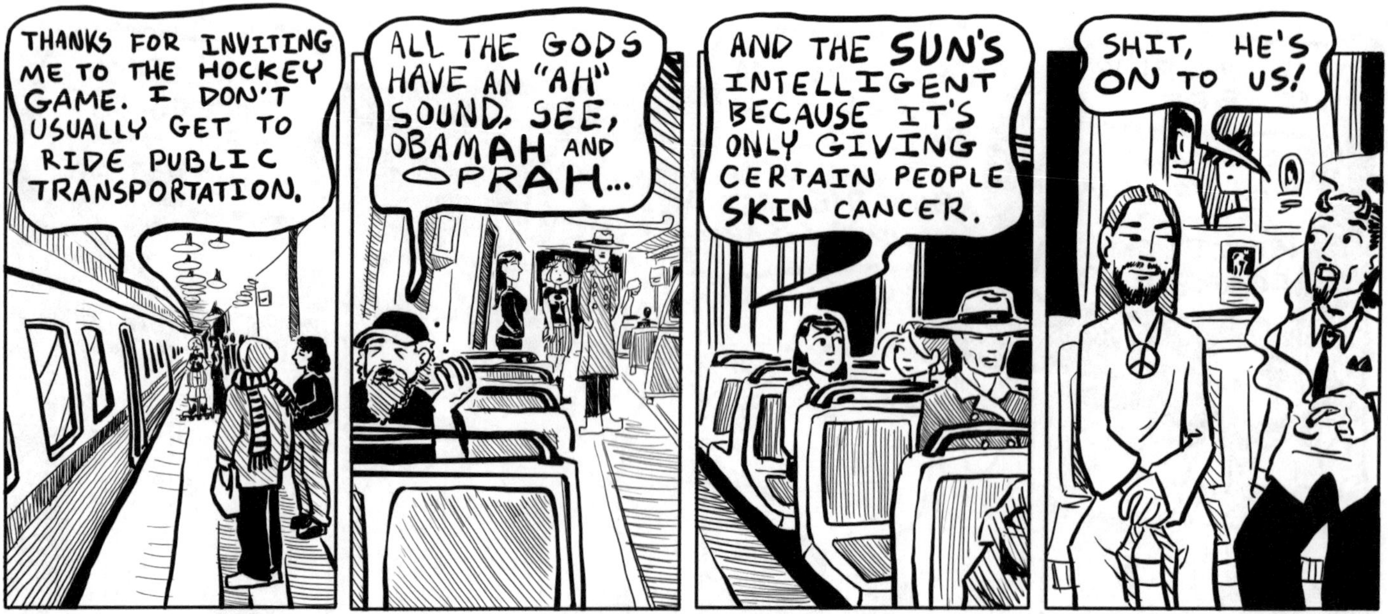
THANKS FOR INVITING ME TO THE HOCKEY GAME. I DON'T USUALLY GET TO RIDE PUBLIC TRANSPORTATION.
ALL THE GODS HAVE AN "AH" SOUND, SEE, OBAMAH AND OPRAH...
AND THE SUN'S INTELLIGENT BECAUSE IT'S ONLY GIVING CERTAIN PEOPLE SKIN CANCER.
SHIT, HE'S ON TO US!

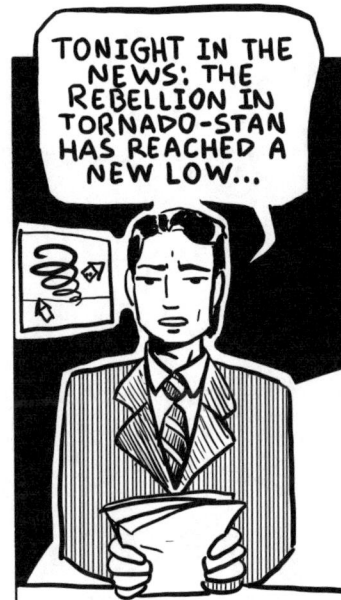

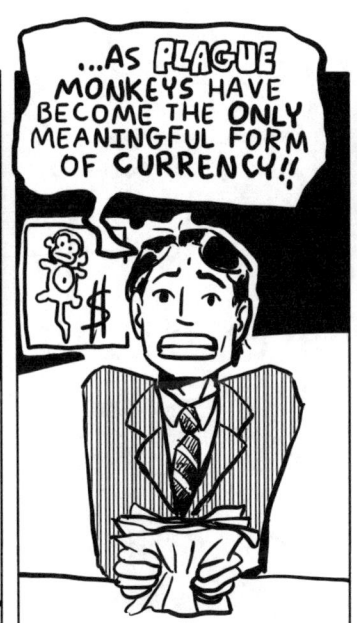

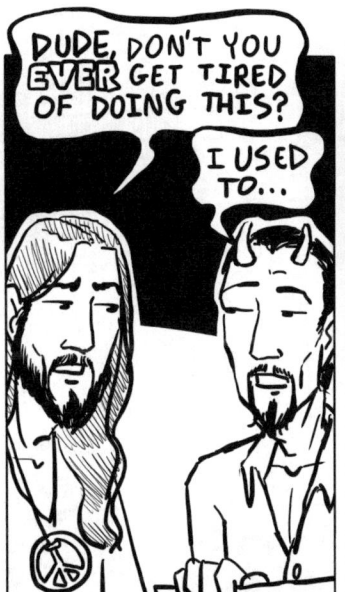

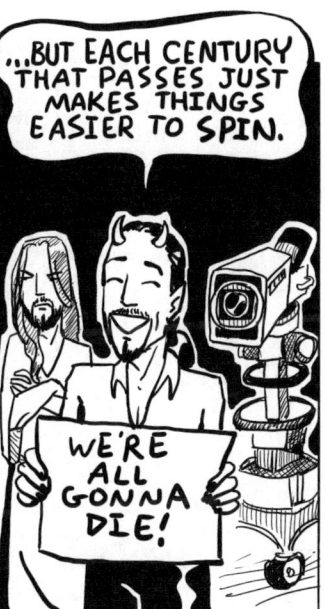

TONIGHT IN THE NEWS: THE REBELLION IN TORNADO-STAN HAS REACHED A NEW LOW...
...AS PLAGUE MONKEYS HAVE BECOME THE ONLY MEANINGFUL FORM OF CURRENCY!!
DUDE, DON'T YOU EVER GET TIRED OF DOING THIS?
I USED TO...
...BUT EACH CENTURY THAT PASSES JUST MAKES THINGS EASIER TO SPIN.
WE'RE ALL GONNA DIE!

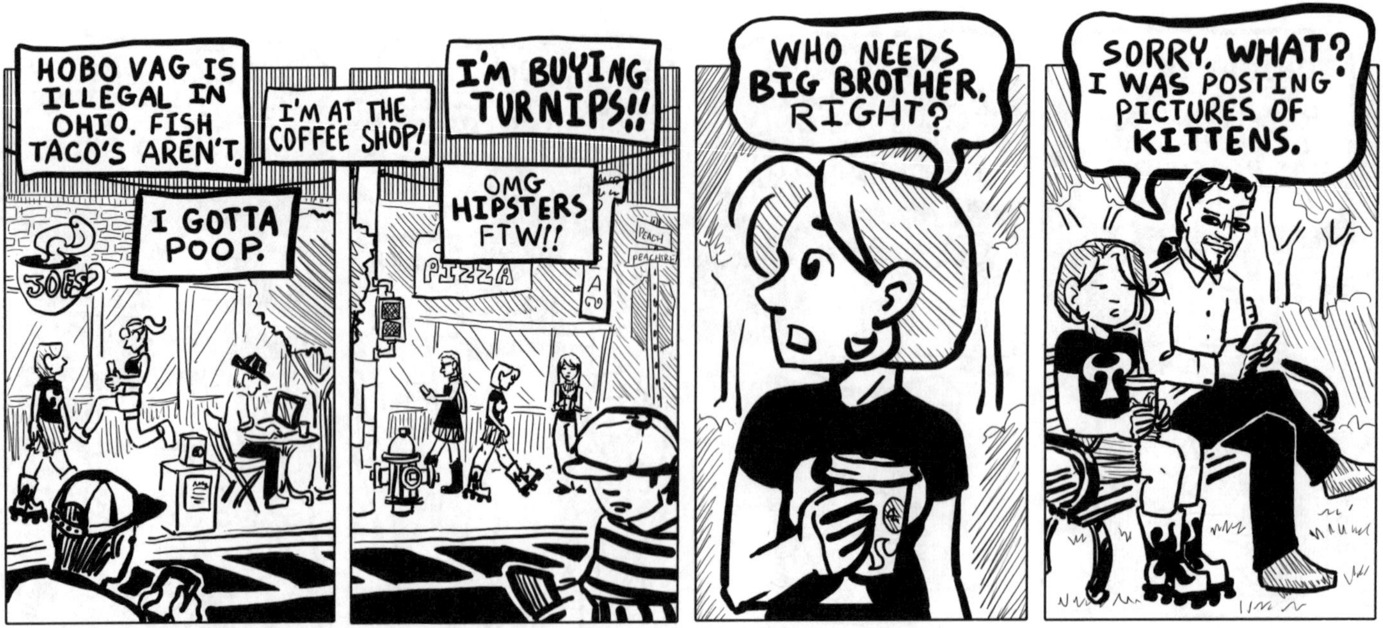
HOBO VAG IS ILLEGAL IN OHIO. FISH TACO'S AREN'T.
I GOTTA POOP.
JOE'S
I'M AT THE COFFEE SHOP!
I'M BUYING TURNIPS!!
OMG HIPSTERS FTW!!
PIZZA
WHO NEEDS BIG BROTHER, RIGHT?
SORRY, WHAT? I WAS POSTING PICTURES OF KITTENS.

WWW.THEDEVILSPANTIES.COM TM JENNIE BREEDEN ©2011

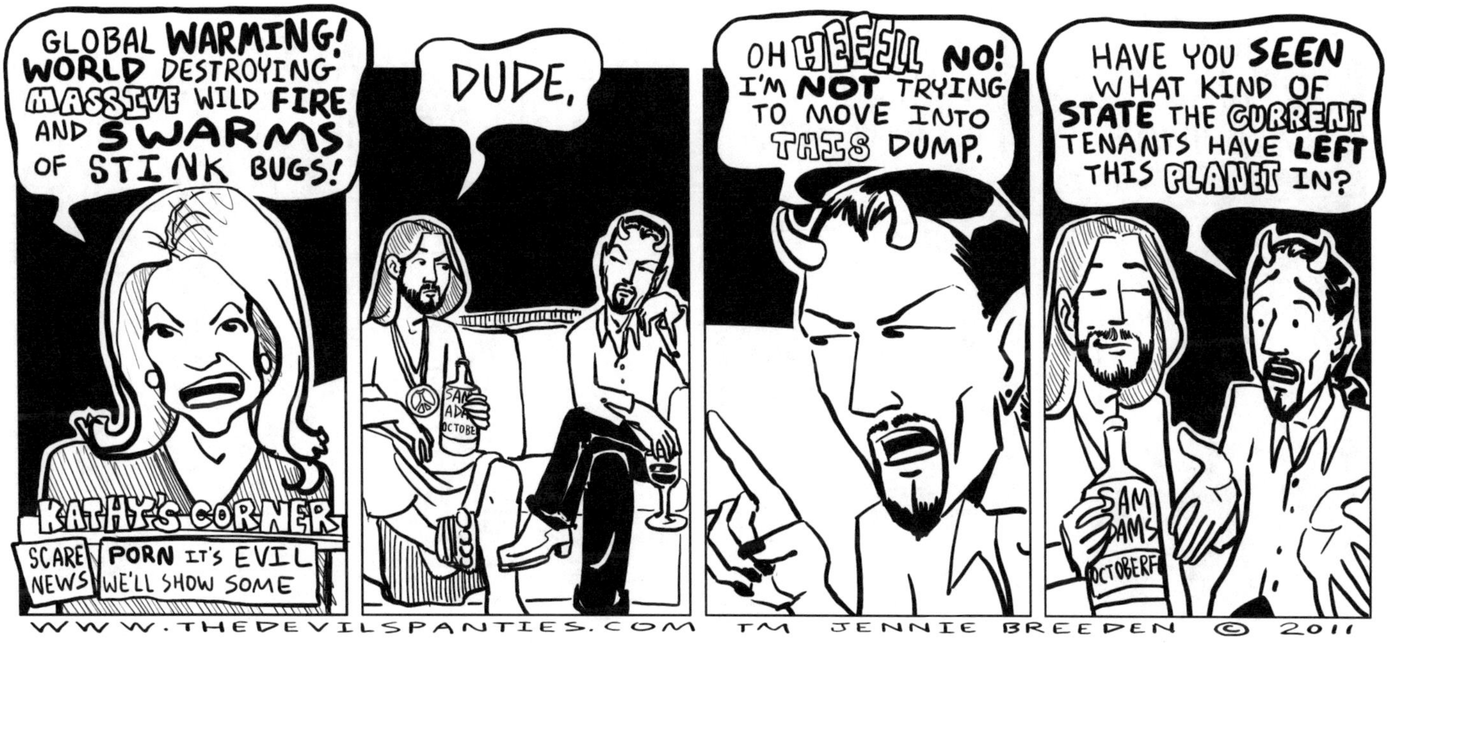
GLOBAL WARMING! WORLD DESTROYING MASSIVE WILD FIRE AND SWARMS OF STINK BUGS!
KATHY'S CORNER
SCARE NEWS
PORN IT'S EVIL WE'LL SHOW SOME
DUDE,
SAM ADA OCTOBE
OH HEEEELL NO! I'M NOT TRYING TO MOVE INTO THIS DUMP.
HAVE YOU SEEN WHAT KIND OF STATE THE CURRENT TENANTS HAVE LEFT THIS PLANET IN?
SAM DAMS OCTOBERF
WWW.THEDEVILSPANTIES.COM TM JENNIE BREEDEN © 2011

HUMANS TREAT THE EARTH LIKE THEIR DAD'S FRAT HOUSE!
THEY SEEM TO EXPECT SOMEONE ELSE WILL COME CLEAN UP AFTER THEM.
THEY ACT LIKE SOMEONE ELSE WILL RESTOCK THE FRIDGE AND PAY THE ELECTRIC BILL.
TRASH
YOU SAYING YOU COULD RUN THE PLACE BETTER?
WHAT DO YOU MEAN COULD?

WWW.THEDEVILSPANTIES.COM TM JENNIE BREEDEN © 2011

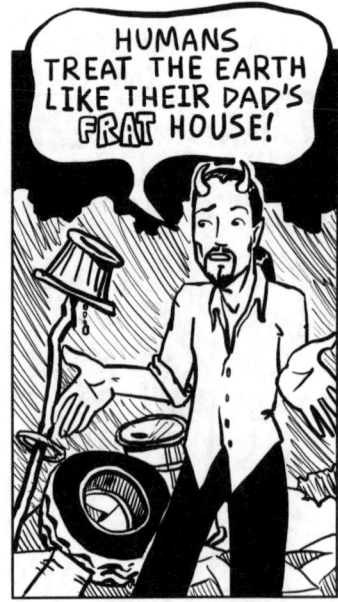

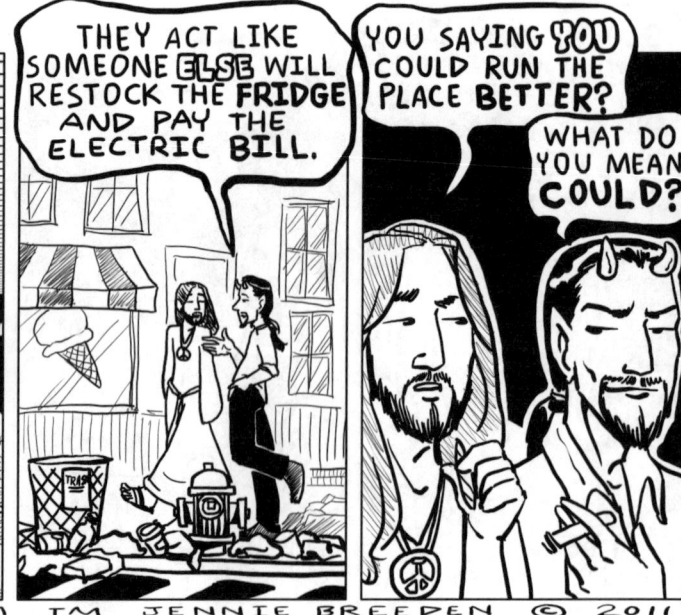

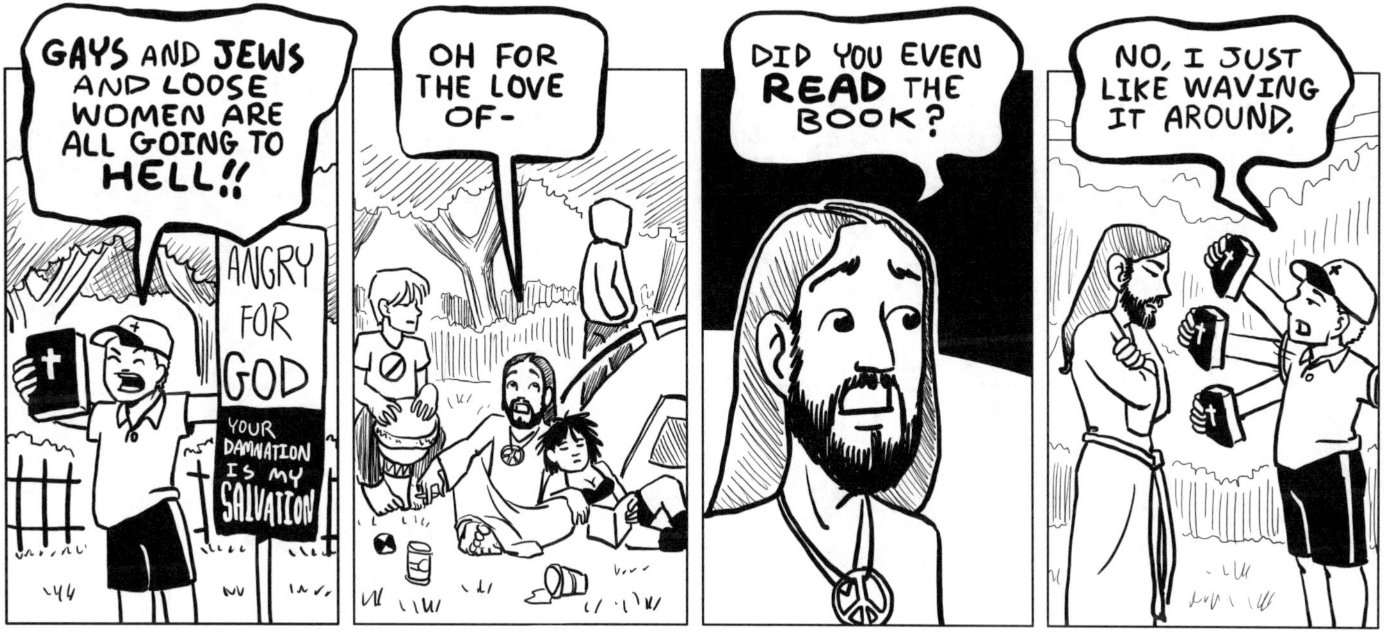
GAYS AND JEWS AND LOOSE WOMEN ARE ALL GOING TO HELL!!
ANGRY FOR GOD
YOUR DAMNATION IS MY SALVATION
OH FOR THE LOVE OF-
DID YOU EVEN READ THE BOOK?
NO, I JUST LIKE WAVING IT AROUND.

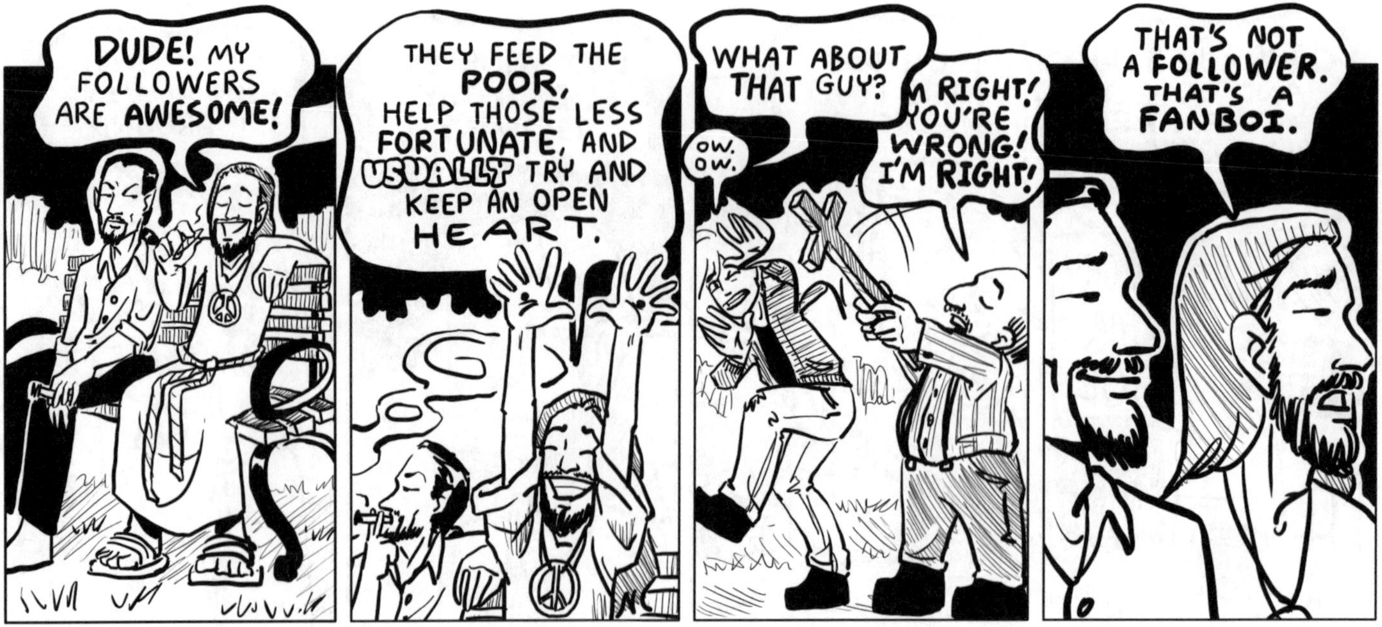
DUDE! MY FOLLOWERS ARE AWESOME!
THEY FEED THE POOR, HELP THOSE LESS FORTUNATE, AND USUALLY TRY AND KEEP AN OPEN HEART.
WHAT ABOUT THAT GUY?
OW. OW.
M RIGHT! YOU'RE WRONG! I'M RIGHT!
THAT'S NOT A FOLLOWER. THAT'S A FANBOI.

JESUS IS COMING, BE PREPARED
BAT GRL
"JESUS IS COMING, BE PREPARED."
OH GOD! TURN YOUR HEAD!
THAT SHIT STINGS IF YOU GET IT IN YOUR EYE.

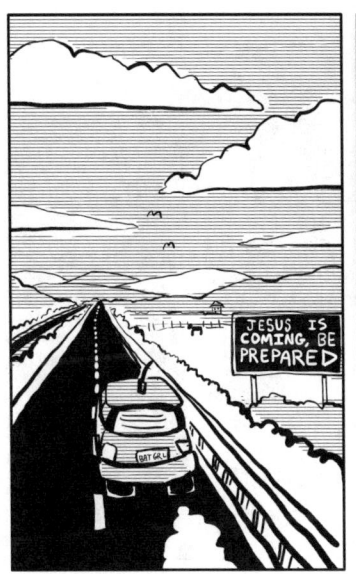

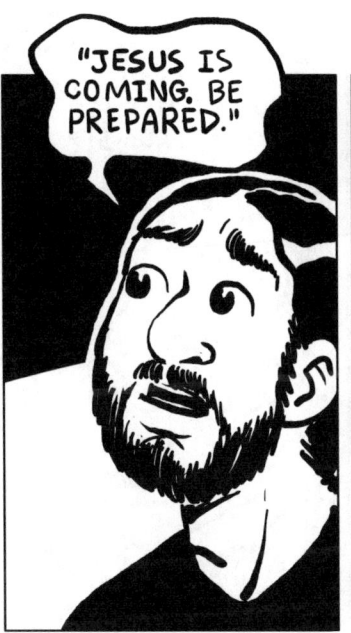

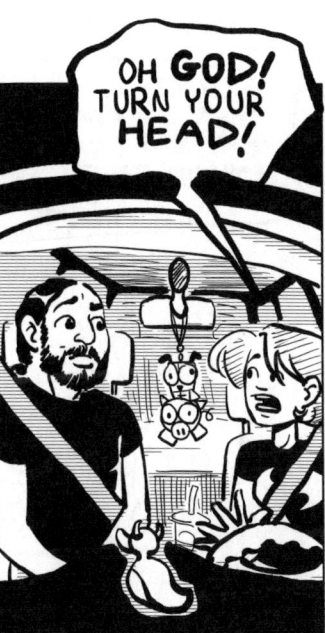

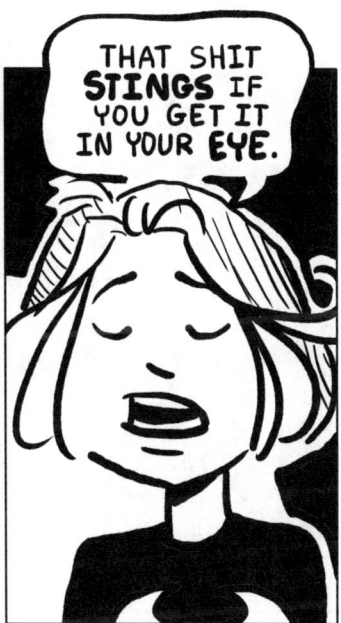

WAIT, SO IF I SAY I'M A DEMOCRAT, THEN I CAN'T CHIME IN ON ABORTION...
SAMPLE BALLOTS
...BUT IF I'M A REPUBLICAN, THEN I CAN'T SAY I'M FOR REDUCING TAXES...
...AND IF I SAY I'M INDEPENDENT, THEN I DON'T GET ANY QUESTIONS!?
THIS IS RETARDED!
YOU'RE AN ASSHAT.
DIVIDE AND CONQUER, BABY.
"VOTE"

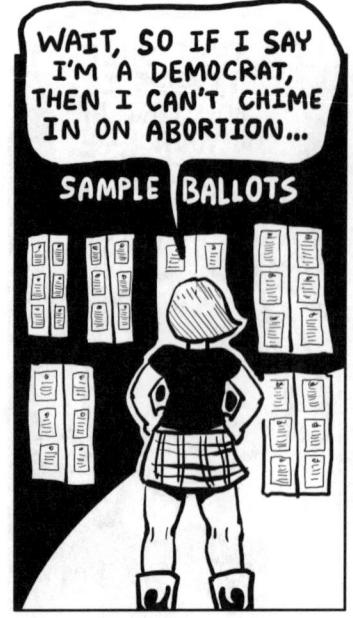

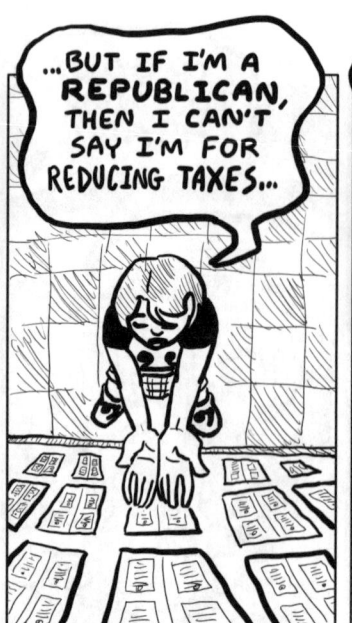

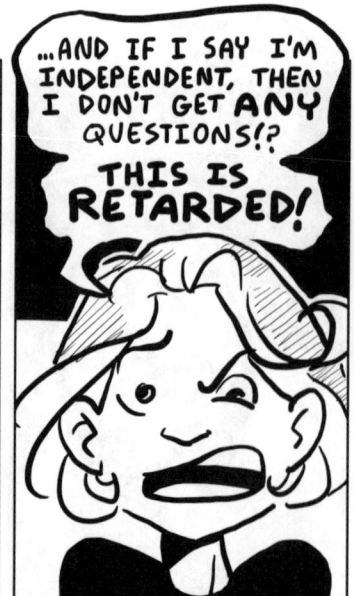

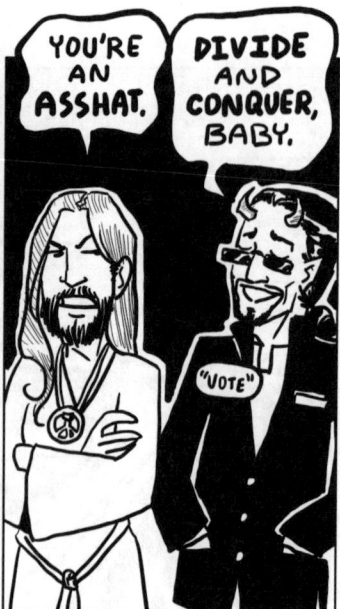

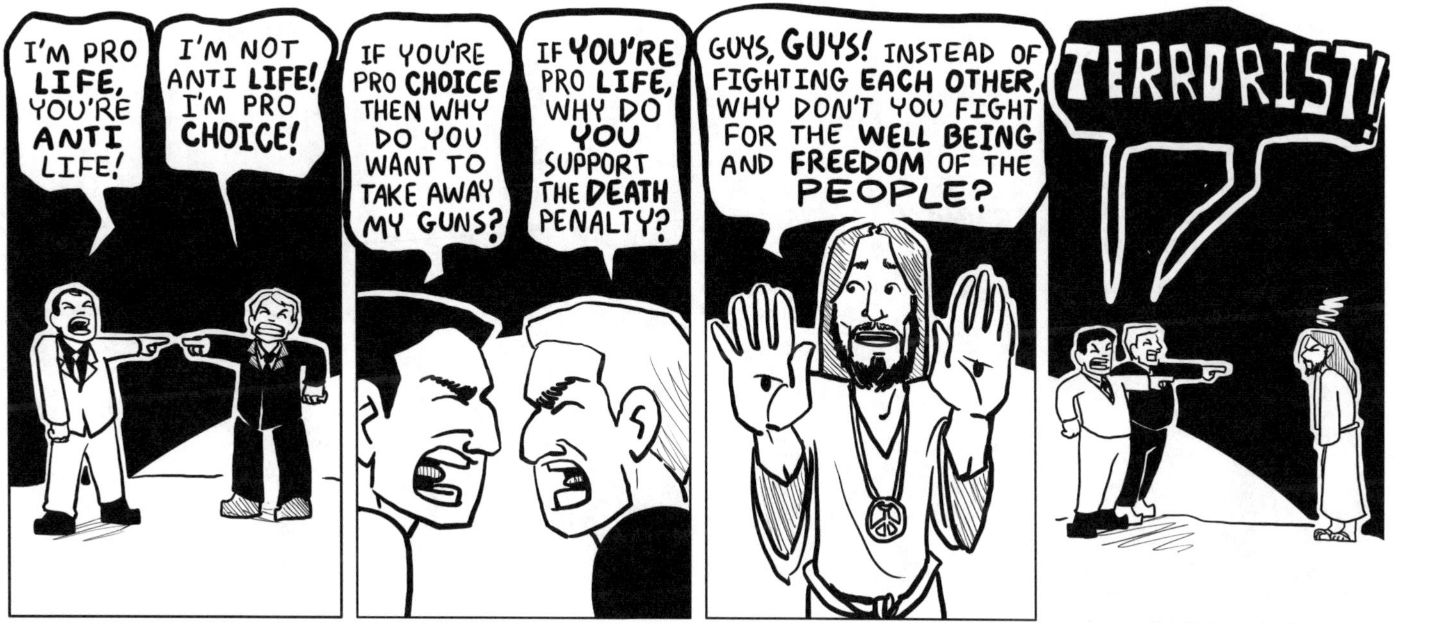
I'M PRO LIFE, YOU'RE ANTI LIFE!
I'M NOT ANTI LIFE! I'M PRO CHOICE!
IF YOU'RE PRO CHOICE THEN WHY DO YOU WANT TO TAKE AWAY MY GUNS?
IF YOU'RE PRO LIFE, WHY DO YOU SUPPORT THE DEATH PENALTY?
GUYS, GUYS! INSTEAD OF FIGHTING EACH OTHER, WHY DON'T YOU FIGHT FOR THE WELL BEING AND FREEDOM OF THE PEOPLE?
TERRORIST!!

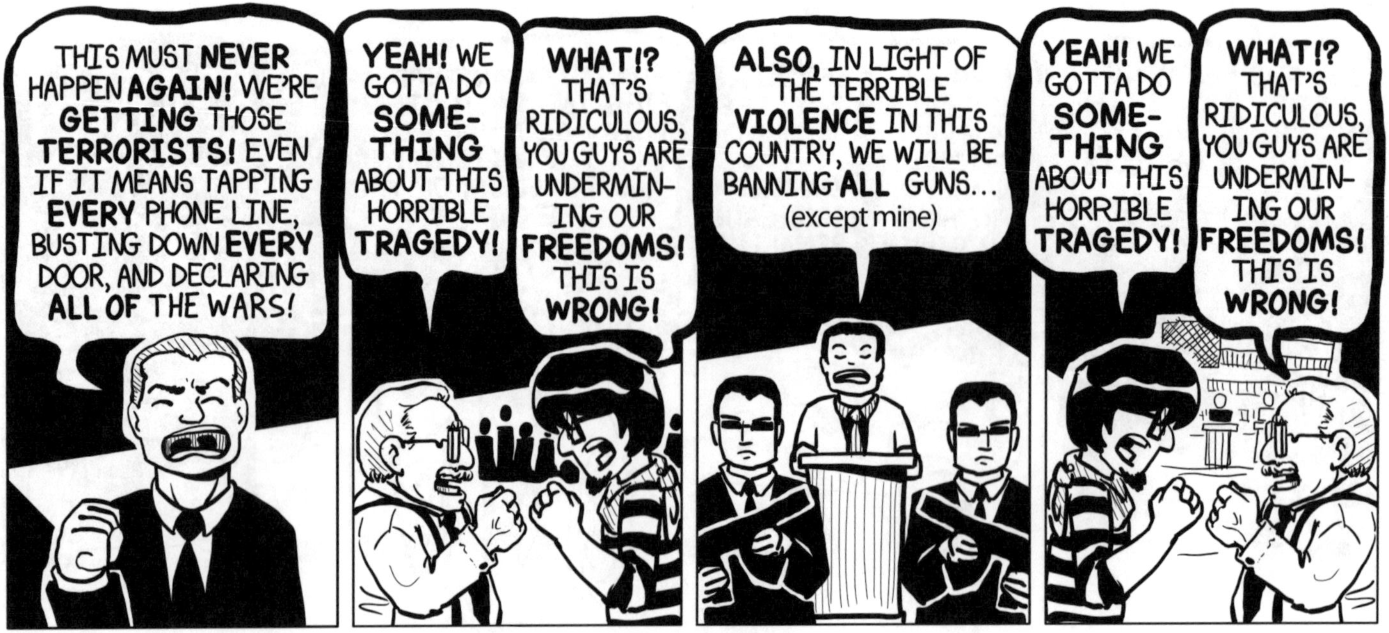
THIS MUST **NEVER** HAPPEN **AGAIN!** WE'RE **GETTING** THOSE **TERRORISTS!** EVEN IF IT MEANS TAPPING **EVERY** PHONE LINE, BUSTING DOWN **EVERY** DOOR, AND DECLARING **ALL OF** THE WARS!
YEAH! WE GOTTA DO **SOME-THING** ABOUT THIS HORRIBLE **TRAGEDY!**
WHAT!? THAT'S RIDICULOUS, YOU GUYS ARE UNDERMIN-ING OUR **FREEDOMS!** THIS IS **WRONG!**
ALSO, IN LIGHT OF THE TERRIBLE **VIOLENCE** IN THIS COUNTRY, WE WILL BE BANNING **ALL** GUNS... (except mine)
YEAH! WE GOTTA DO **SOME-THING** ABOUT THIS HORRIBLE **TRAGEDY!**
WHAT!? THAT'S RIDICULOUS, YOU GUYS ARE UNDERMIN-ING OUR **FREEDOMS!** THIS IS **WRONG!**

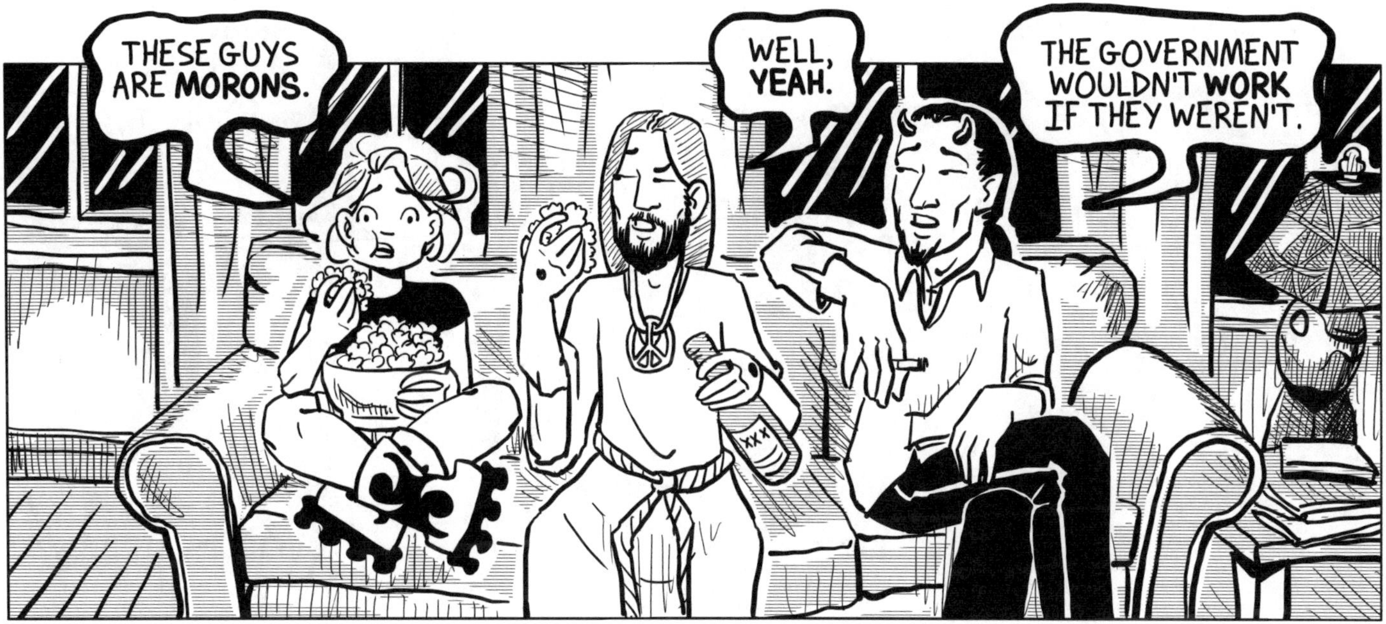
THESE GUYS ARE MORONS.
WELL, YEAH.
THE GOVERNMENT WOULDN'T WORK IF THEY WEREN'T.

DUDE, WE GOTTA **TALK.**
NATURALLY.
THIS HAS GONE A **BIT** TOO FAR...
NEWS
YOU THINK YOU COULD GET YOUR FOLLOWERS TO STOP USING PICTURES OF **DISASTER** VICTIMS TO PUSH THEIR AGENDAS?
"**DUDE**", I HAVE ABOUT AS MUCH CONTROL OVER MY FOLLOWERS AS YOU DO OVER YOURS.

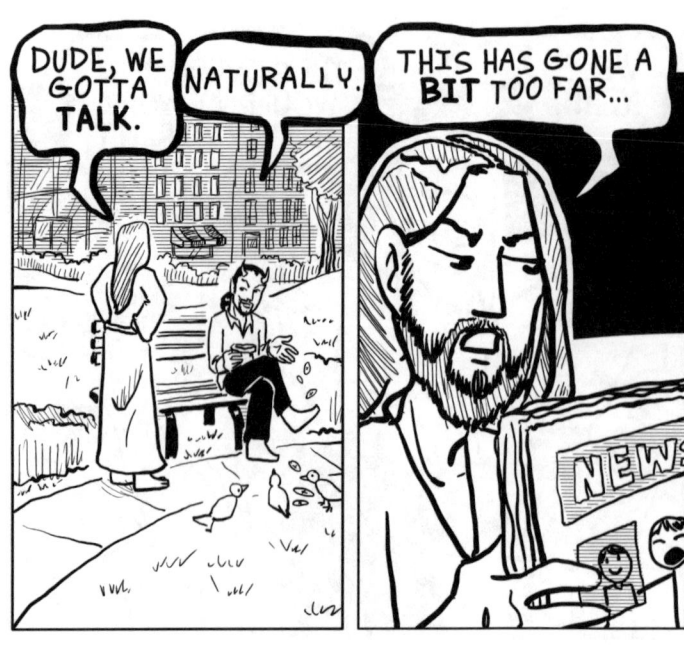

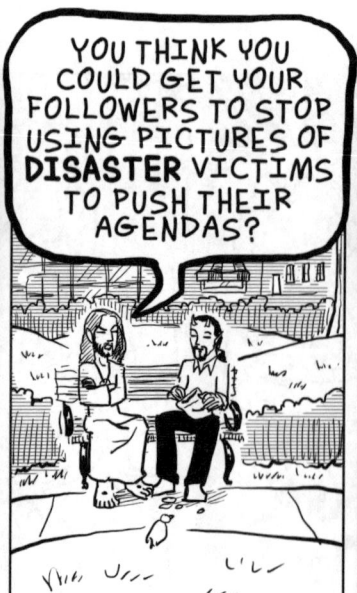

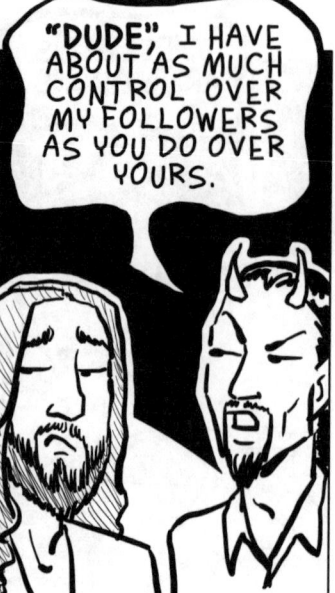

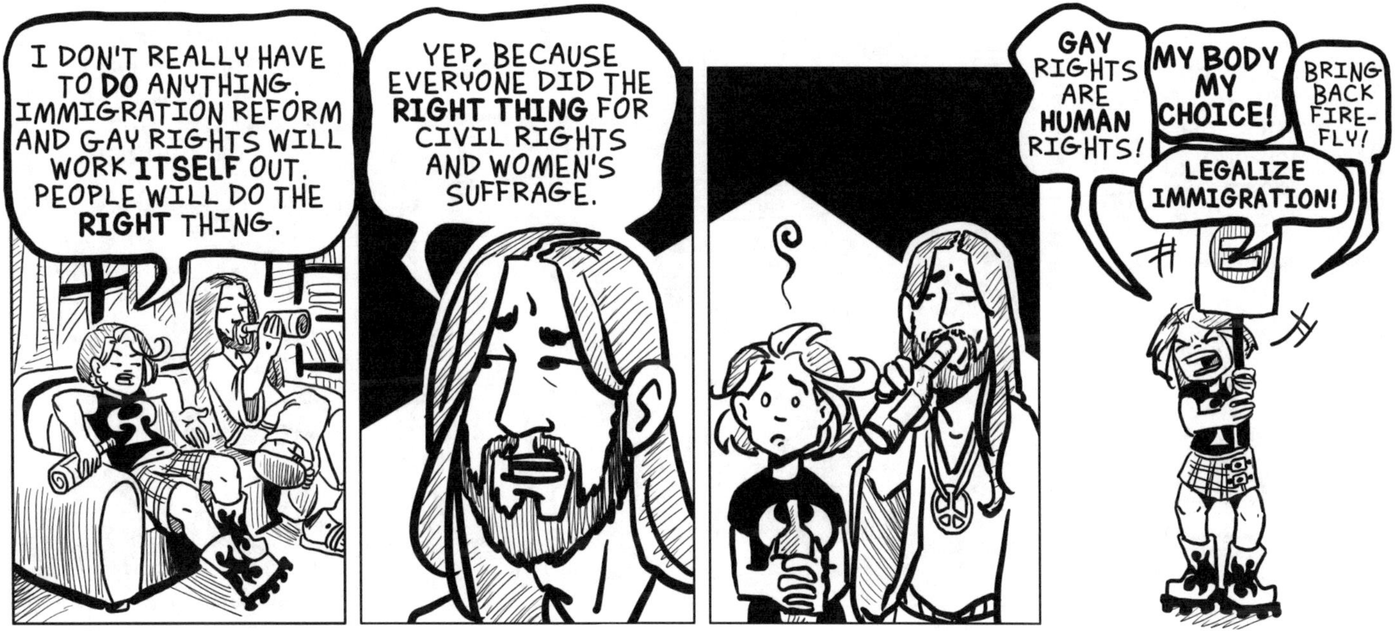
I DON'T REALLY HAVE TO **DO** ANYTHING. IMMIGRATION REFORM AND GAY RIGHTS WILL WORK **ITSELF** OUT. PEOPLE WILL DO THE **RIGHT** THING.
YEP, BECAUSE EVERYONE DID THE **RIGHT THING** FOR CIVIL RIGHTS AND WOMEN'S SUFFRAGE.
GAY RIGHTS ARE HUMAN RIGHTS!
MY BODY MY CHOICE!
BRING BACK FIRE-FLY!
LEGALIZE IMMIGRATION!

THE POPE DECLARED TODAY THAT WE SHOULDN'T JUDGE GAY PEOPLE, THAT THE CHURCH SHOULD HELP THE POOR, AND THAT ATHIESTS ARE A OK!
...WHAT?
...I DIDN'T DO ANYTHING!
OKAY, OKAY, WE'VE TOTALLY PULLED OUR AGENTS OUT OF THE CHURCH.

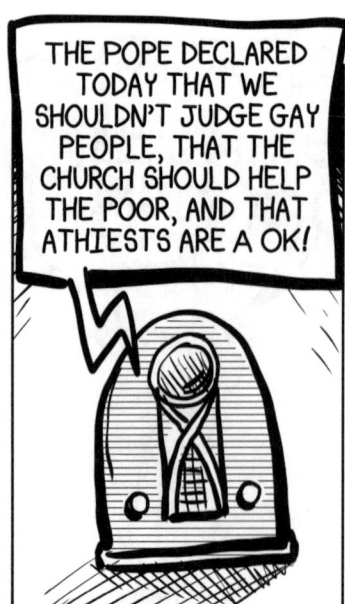

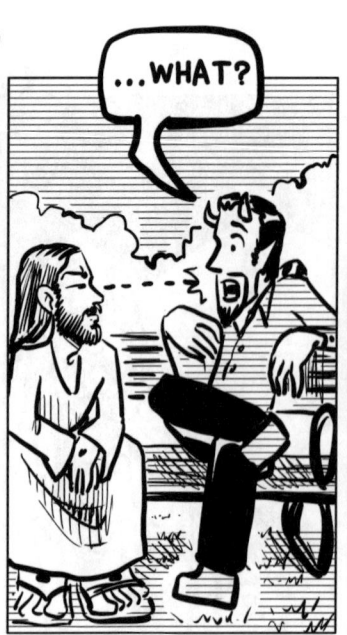

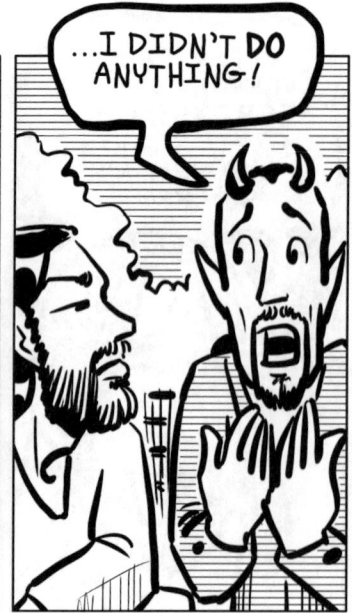

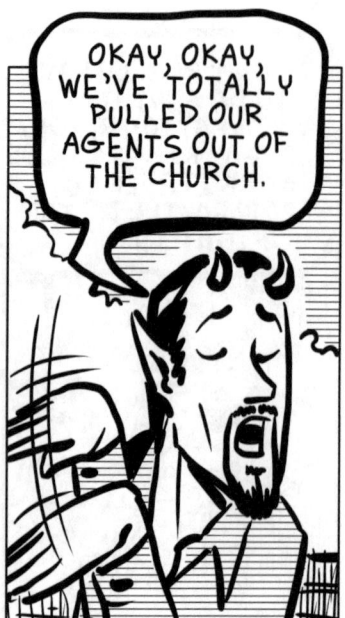

IT WAS TOO MUCH **OVERHEAD.** TOO HIGH COST, HIGH RISK, LOW **RETURN.** TOO MANY RESOURCES FOR NOT ENOUGH **GAIN.**
....
OKAY, SO WE MOVED THEM ALL OVER TO **POLITICS.**
MUCH EASIER. THOSE GUYS JUST **LINE UP** AT MY DOOR!

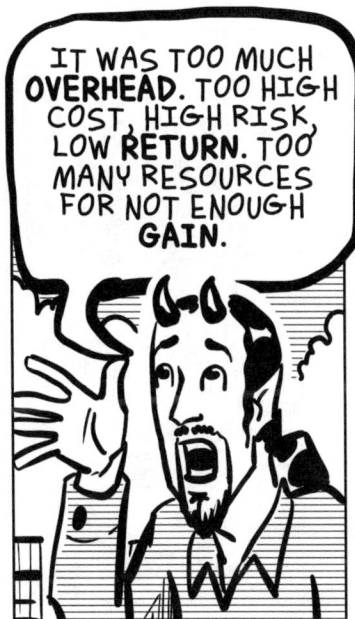

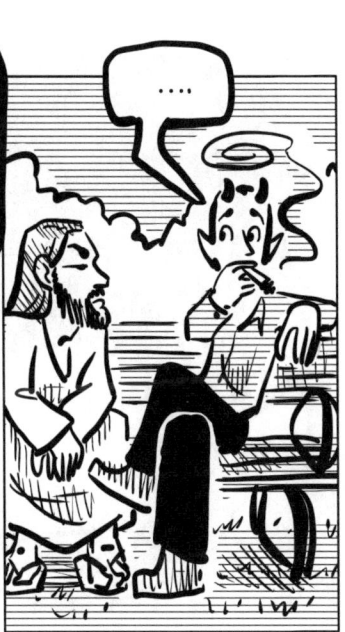

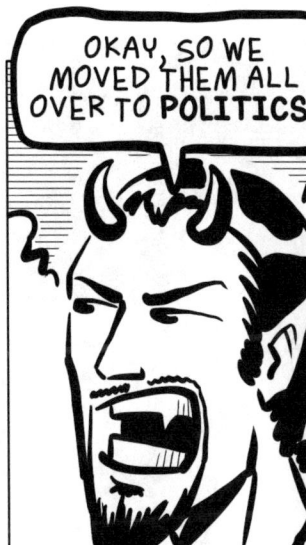

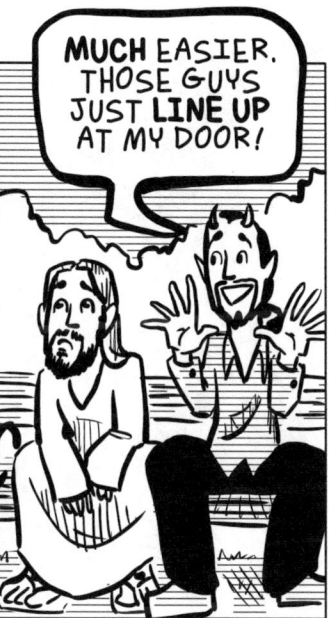

RECORD SHATERING STORMS, FLOODS, AND BLIZARDS. **WHAT** GLOBAL WARMING?
SOMETIMES I WISH I COULD TURN WATER INTO **VODKA.**

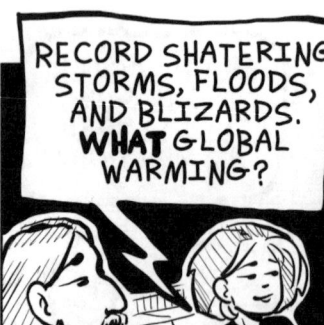

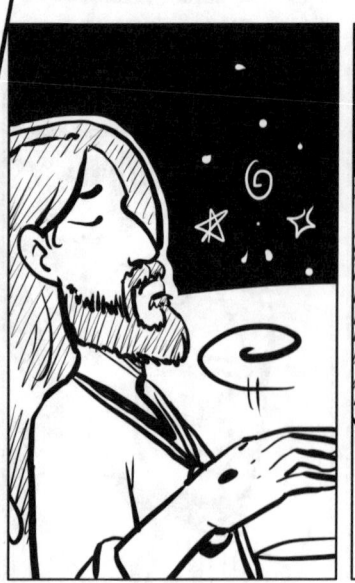

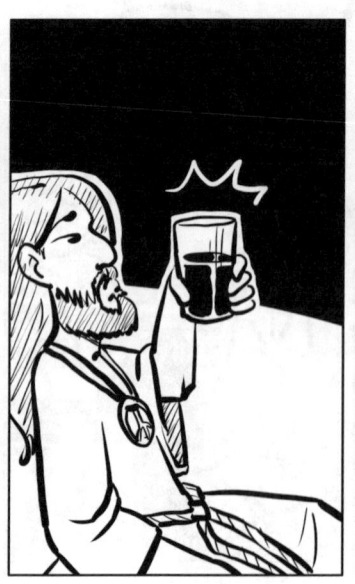

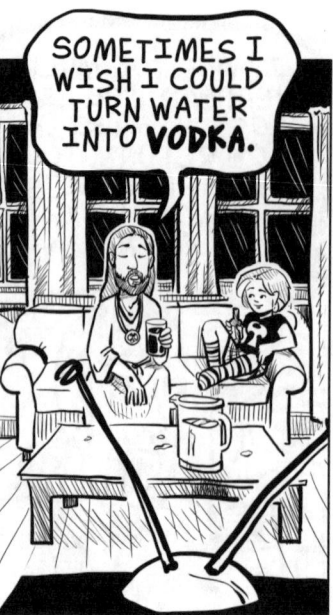

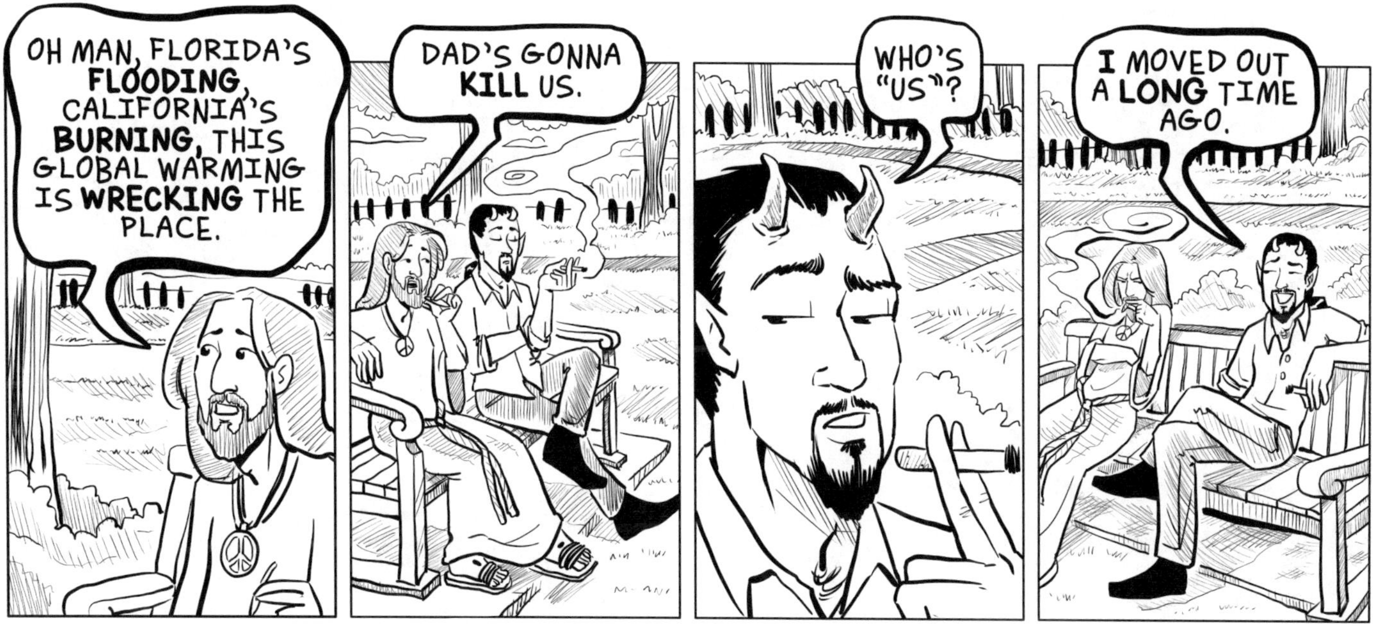
OH MAN, FLORIDA'S **FLOODING**, CALIFORNIA'S **BURNING**, THIS GLOBAL WARMING IS **WRECKING** THE PLACE.
DAD'S GONNA **KILL** US.
WHO'S "US"?
I MOVED OUT A **LONG** TIME AGO.

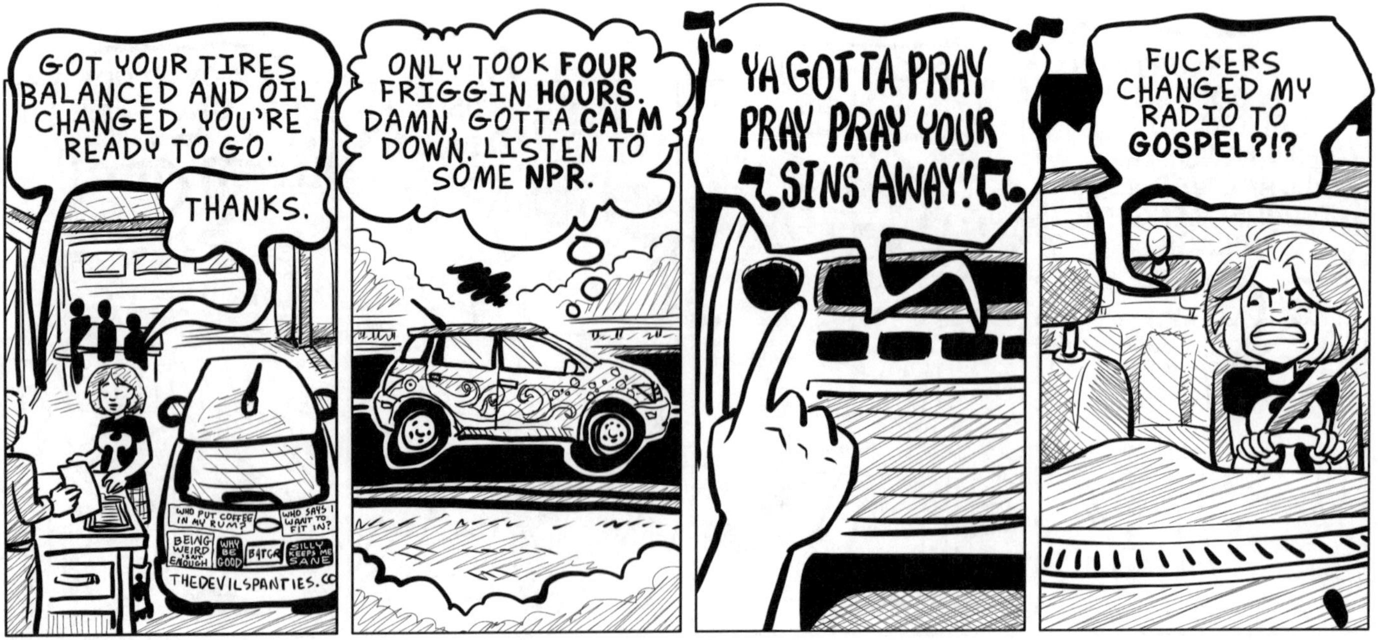
GOT YOUR TIRES BALANCED AND OIL CHANGED. YOU'RE READY TO GO.
THANKS.
WHO PUT COFFEE IN MY RUM?
WHO SAYS I WANT TO FIT IN?
WHY BE GOOD
SILLY KEEPS ME SANE
THEDEVILSPANTIES.CO
ONLY TOOK **FOUR** FRIGGIN **HOURS.** DAMN, GOTTA **CALM** DOWN. LISTEN TO SOME **NPR.**
YA GOTTA PRAY PRAY PRAY YOUR SINS AWAY!
FUCKERS CHANGED MY RADIO TO **GOSPEL?!?**

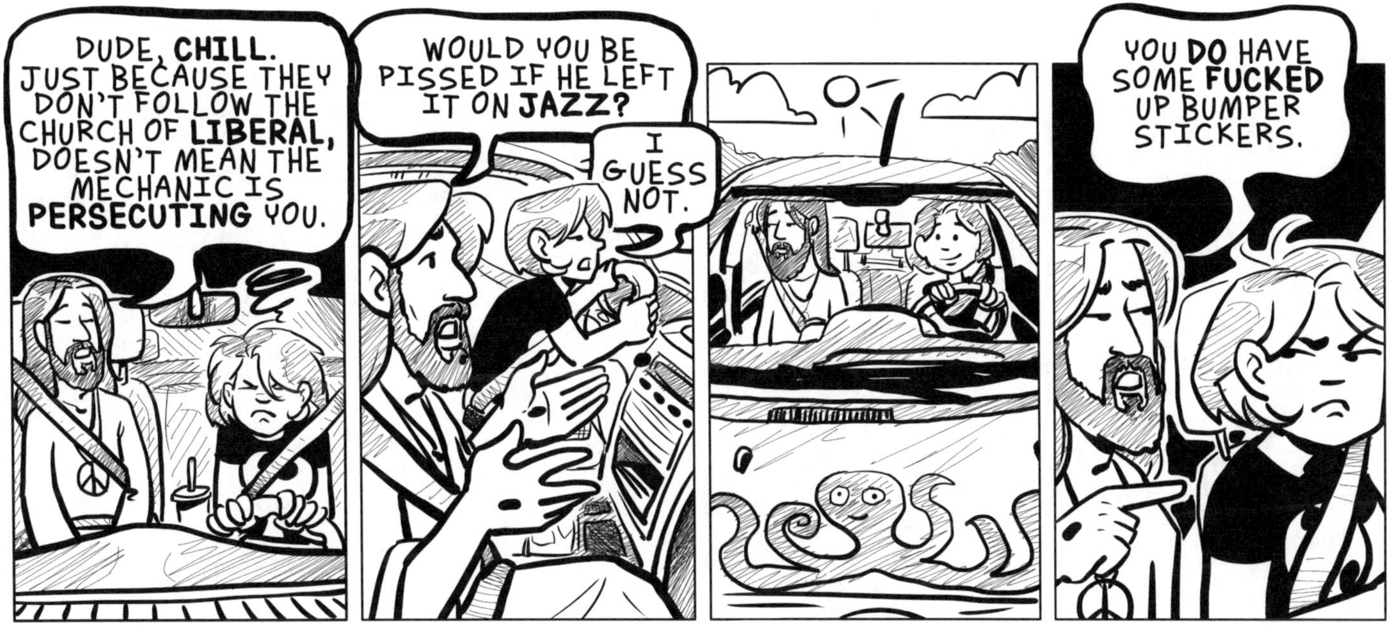
DUDE, **CHILL.** JUST BECAUSE THEY DON'T FOLLOW THE CHURCH OF **LIBERAL,** DOESN'T MEAN THE MECHANIC IS **PERSECUTING** YOU.
WOULD YOU BE PISSED IF HE LEFT IT ON **JAZZ?**
I GUESS NOT.
YOU **DO** HAVE SOME **FUCKED** UP BUMPER STICKERS.

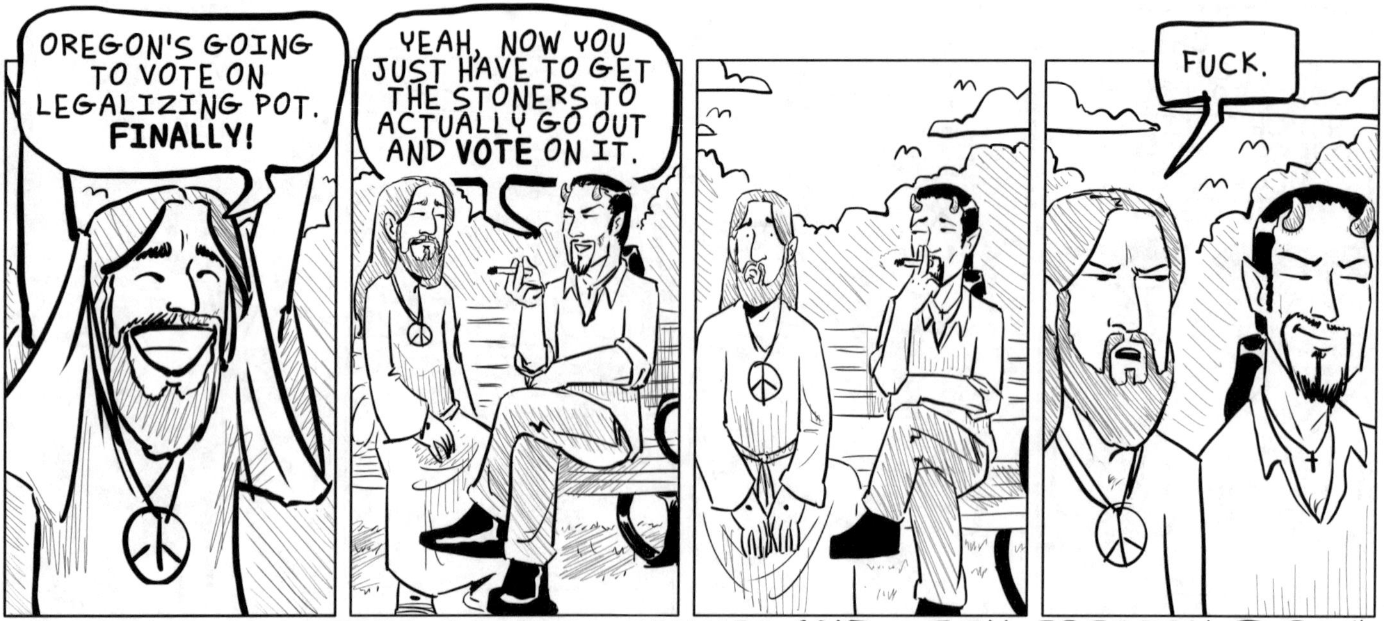
OREGON'S GOING TO VOTE ON LEGALIZING POT. **FINALLY!**
YEAH, NOW YOU JUST HAVE TO GET THE STONERS TO ACTUALLY GO OUT AND **VOTE** ON IT.
FUCK.

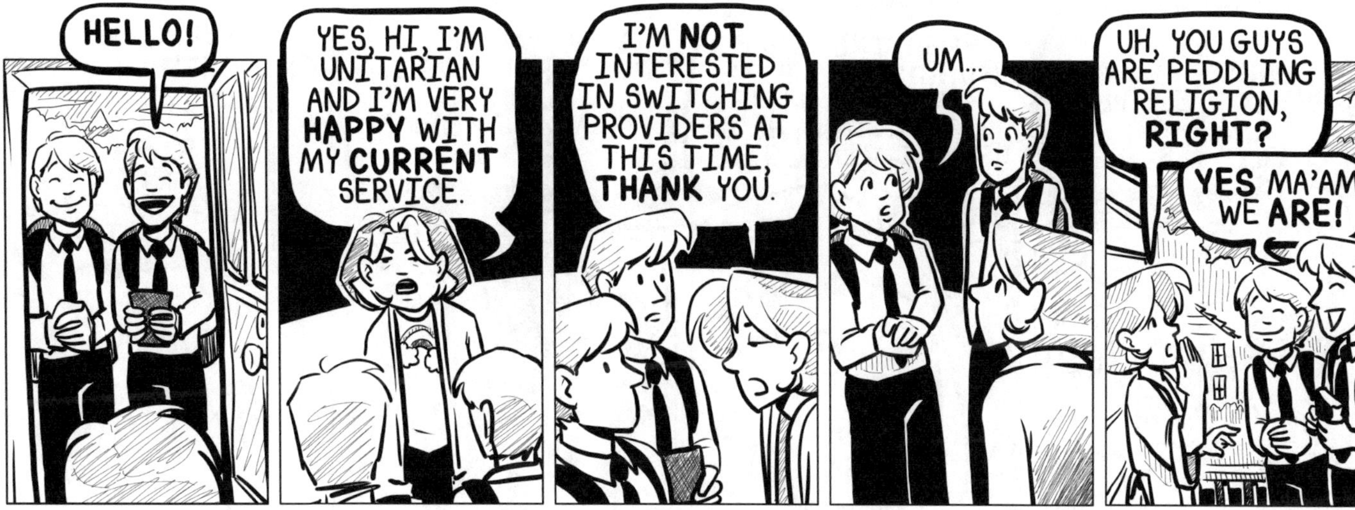
HELLO!
YES, HI, I'M UNITARIAN AND I'M VERY **HAPPY** WITH MY **CURRENT** SERVICE.
I'M **NOT** INTERESTED IN SWITCHING PROVIDERS AT THIS TIME, **THANK** YOU.
UM...
UH, YOU GUYS ARE PEDDLING RELIGION, **RIGHT?**
YES MA'AM, WE **ARE!**

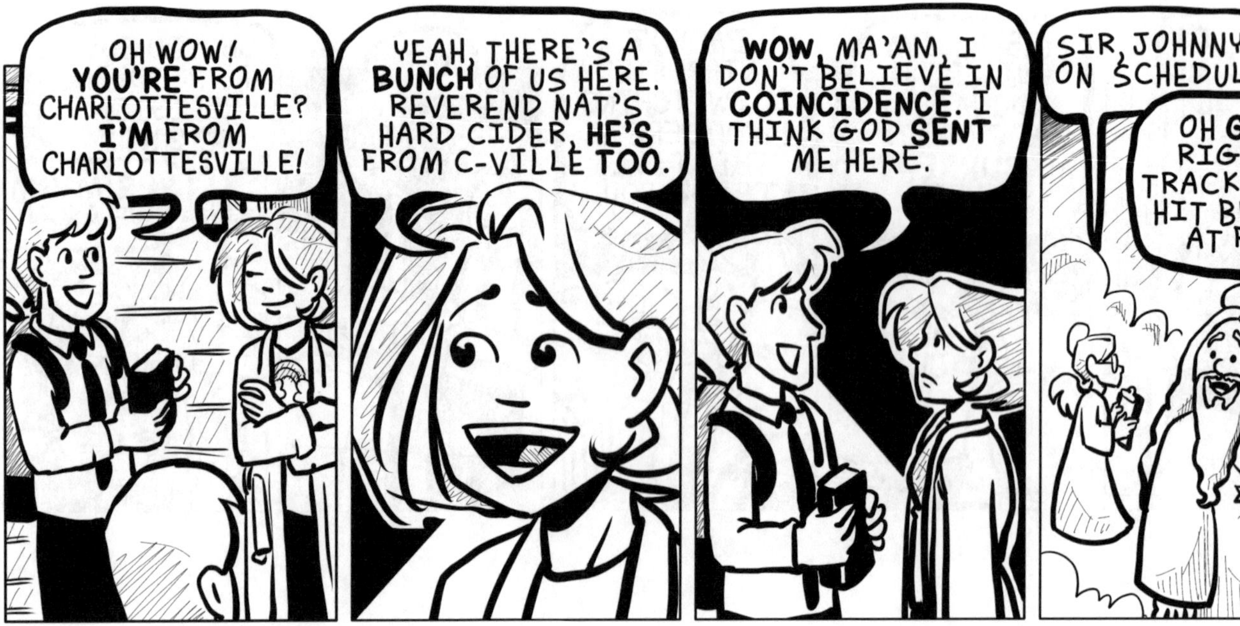
OH WOW! YOU'RE FROM CHARLOTTESVILLE? I'M FROM CHARLOTTESVILLE!
YEAH, THERE'S A BUNCH OF US HERE. REVEREND NAT'S HARD CIDER, HE'S FROM C-VILLE TOO.
WOW, MA'AM, I DON'T BELIEVE IN COINCIDENCE. I THINK GOD SENT ME HERE.
SIR, JOHNNY'S ON SCHEDULE.
OH GOOD, RIGHT ON TRACK TO GET HIT BY A BUS AT FIVE.

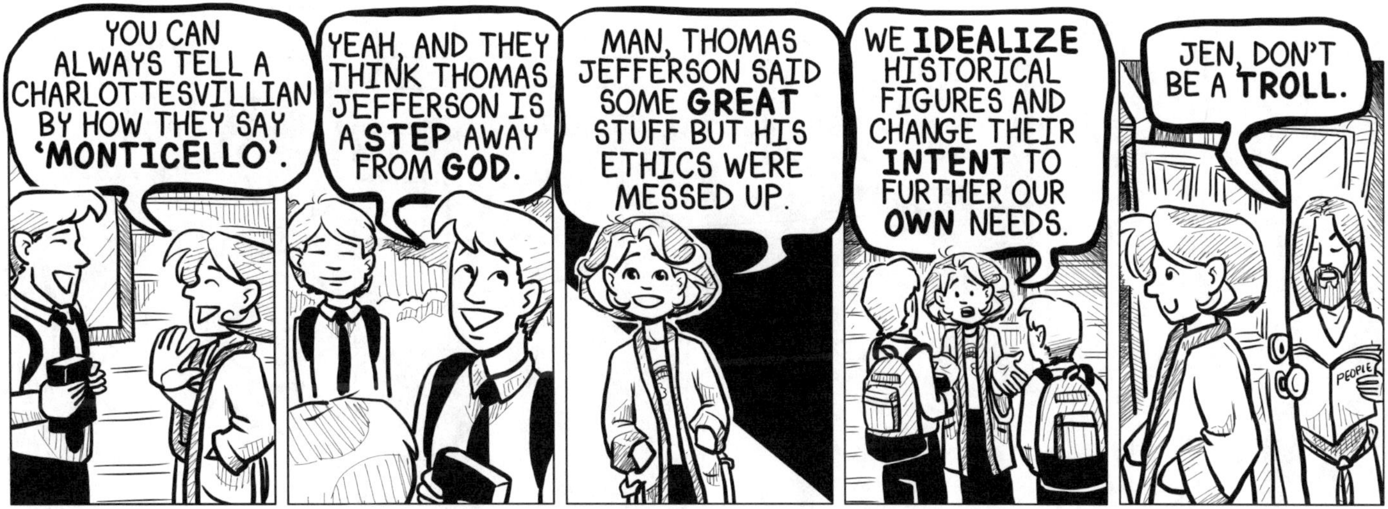

YOU CAN ALWAYS TELL A CHARLOTTESVILLIAN BY HOW THEY SAY 'MONTICELLO'.
YEAH, AND THEY THINK THOMAS JEFFERSON IS A STEP AWAY FROM GOD.
MAN, THOMAS JEFFERSON SAID SOME GREAT STUFF BUT HIS ETHICS WERE MESSED UP.
WE IDEALIZE HISTORICAL FIGURES AND CHANGE THEIR INTENT TO FURTHER OUR OWN NEEDS.
JEN, DON'T BE A TROLL.
PEOPLE

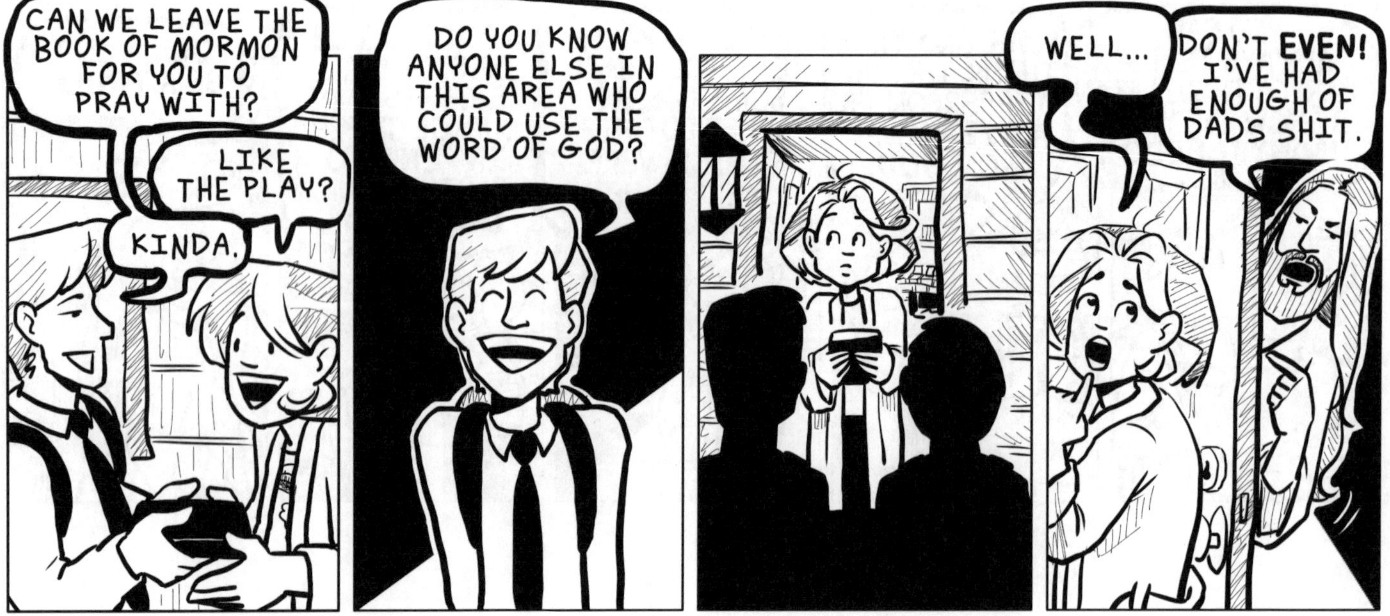
CAN WE LEAVE THE BOOK OF MORMON FOR YOU TO PRAY WITH?
LIKE THE PLAY?
KINDA.
DO YOU KNOW ANYONE ELSE IN THIS AREA WHO COULD USE THE WORD OF GOD?
WELL...
DON'T **EVEN!** I'VE HAD ENOUGH OF DADS SHIT.

I began the comic in 2001. In 2004 I printed the first book and realized I hadn't saved the first year at a high enough resolution for printing. This lead me to re-draw all of the first year. The following comics are the original strips that were posted in 2001 along with their updated versions.

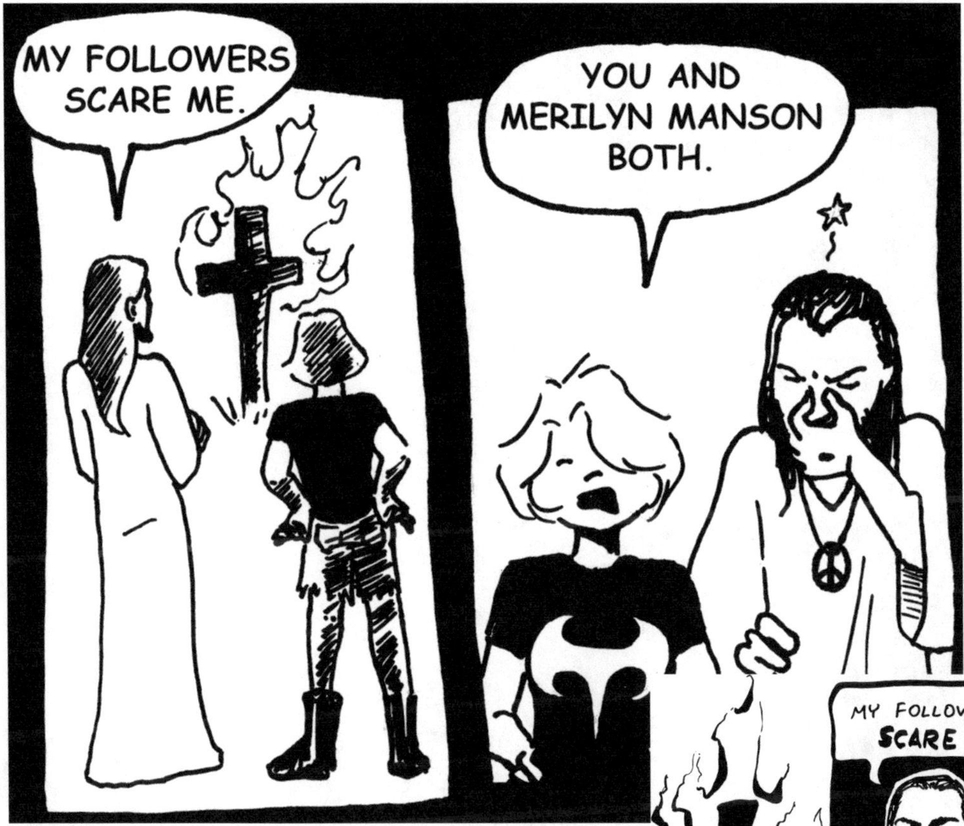
MY FOLLOWERS SCARE ME.
YOU AND MERILYN MANSON BOTH.

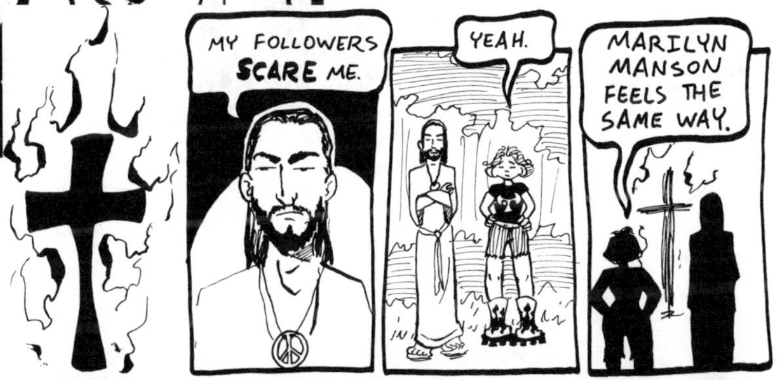
MY FOLLOWERS SCARE ME.
YEAH.
MARILYN MANSON FEELS THE SAME WAY.

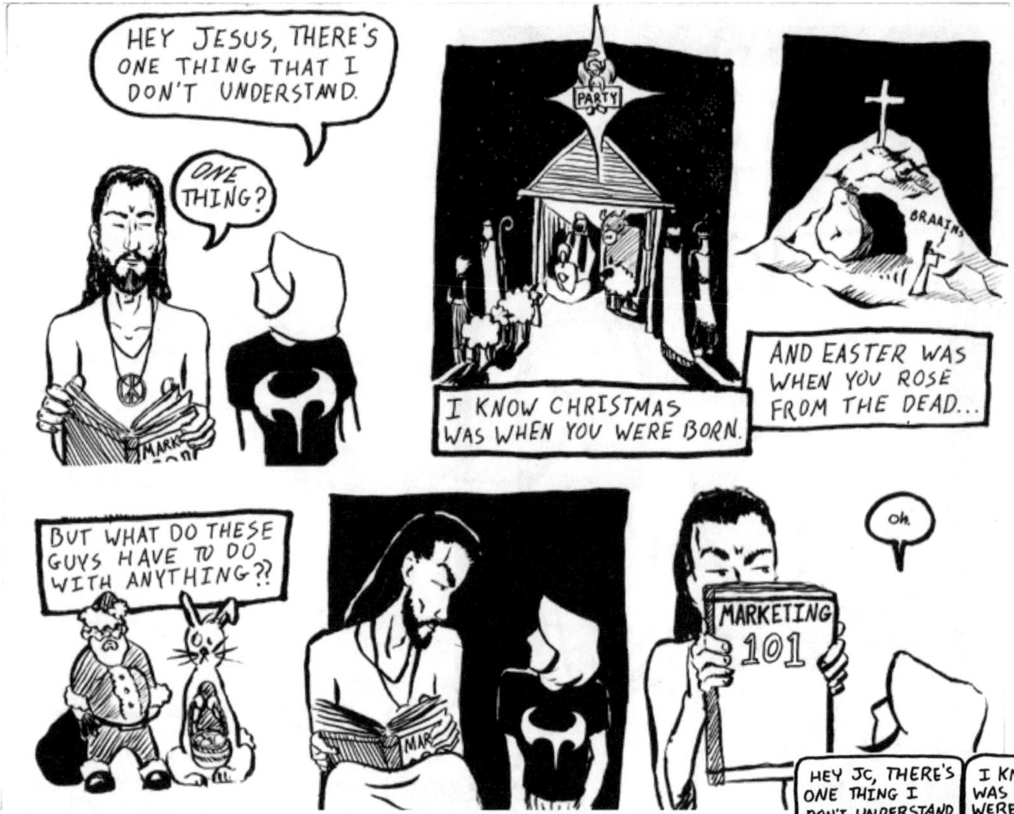

HEY JESUS, THERE'S ONE THING THAT I DON'T UNDERSTAND.
ONE THING?
PARTY
I KNOW CHRISTMAS WAS WHEN YOU WERE BORN.
BRAAINS
AND EASTER WAS WHEN YOU ROSE FROM THE DEAD...
BUT WHAT DO THESE GUYS HAVE TO DO WITH ANYTHING??
oh.
MARKETING 101

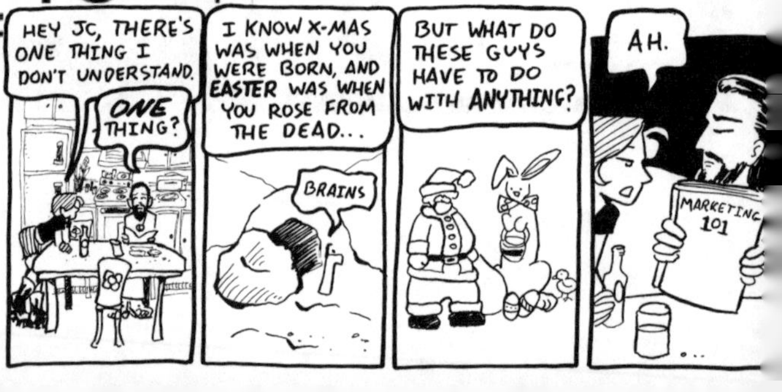

HEY JC, THERE'S ONE THING I DON'T UNDERSTAND.
ONE THING?
I KNOW X-MAS WAS WHEN YOU WERE BORN, AND EASTER WAS WHEN YOU ROSE FROM THE DEAD...
BRAINS
BUT WHAT DO THESE GUYS HAVE TO DO WITH ANYTHING?
AH.
MARKETING 101

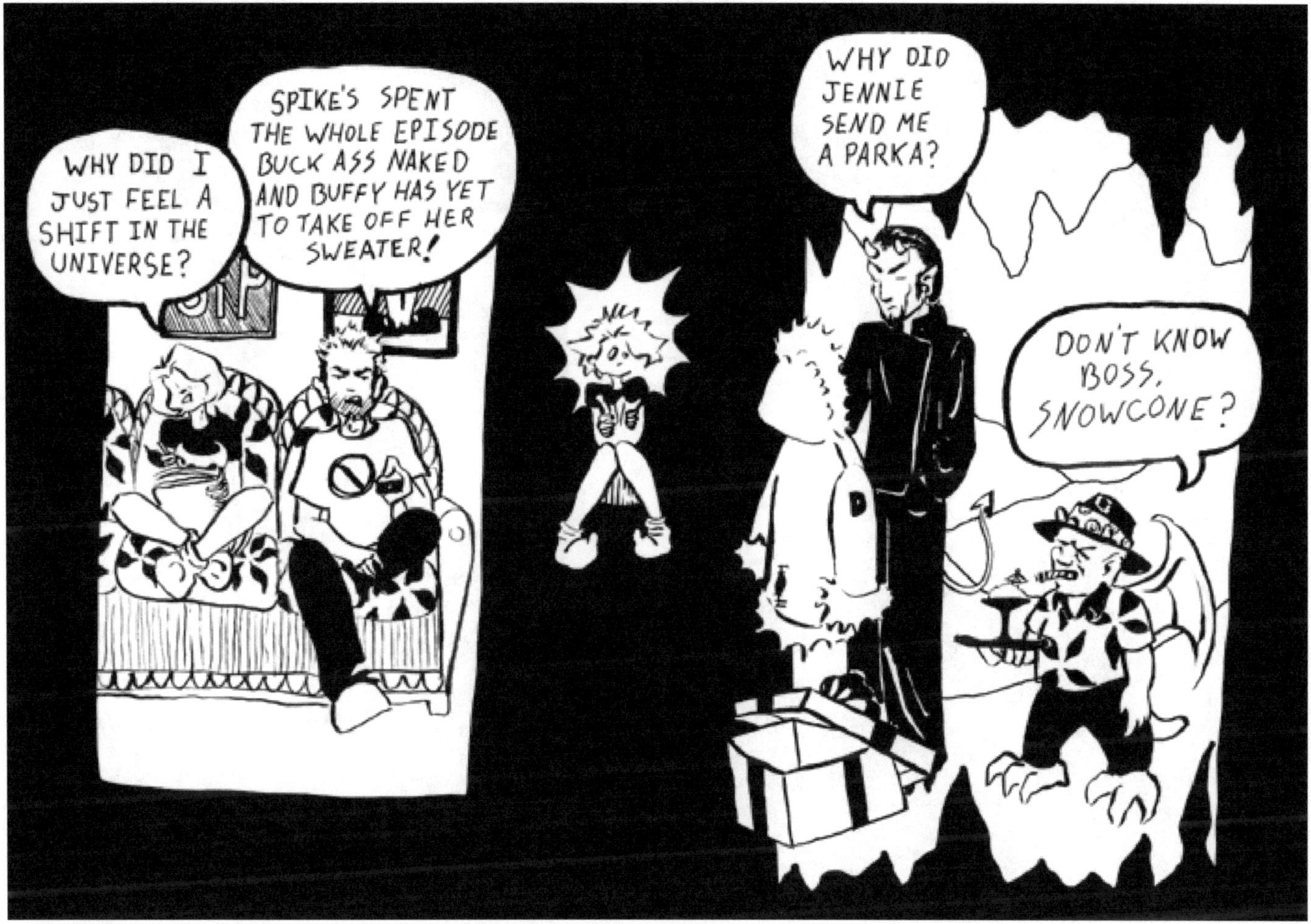

WHY DID I JUST FEEL A SHIFT IN THE UNIVERSE?
SPIKE'S SPENT THE WHOLE EPISODE BUCK ASS NAKED AND BUFFY HAS YET TO TAKE OFF HER SWEATER!
WHY DID JENNIE SEND ME A PARKA?
DON'T KNOW BOSS. SNOWCONE?

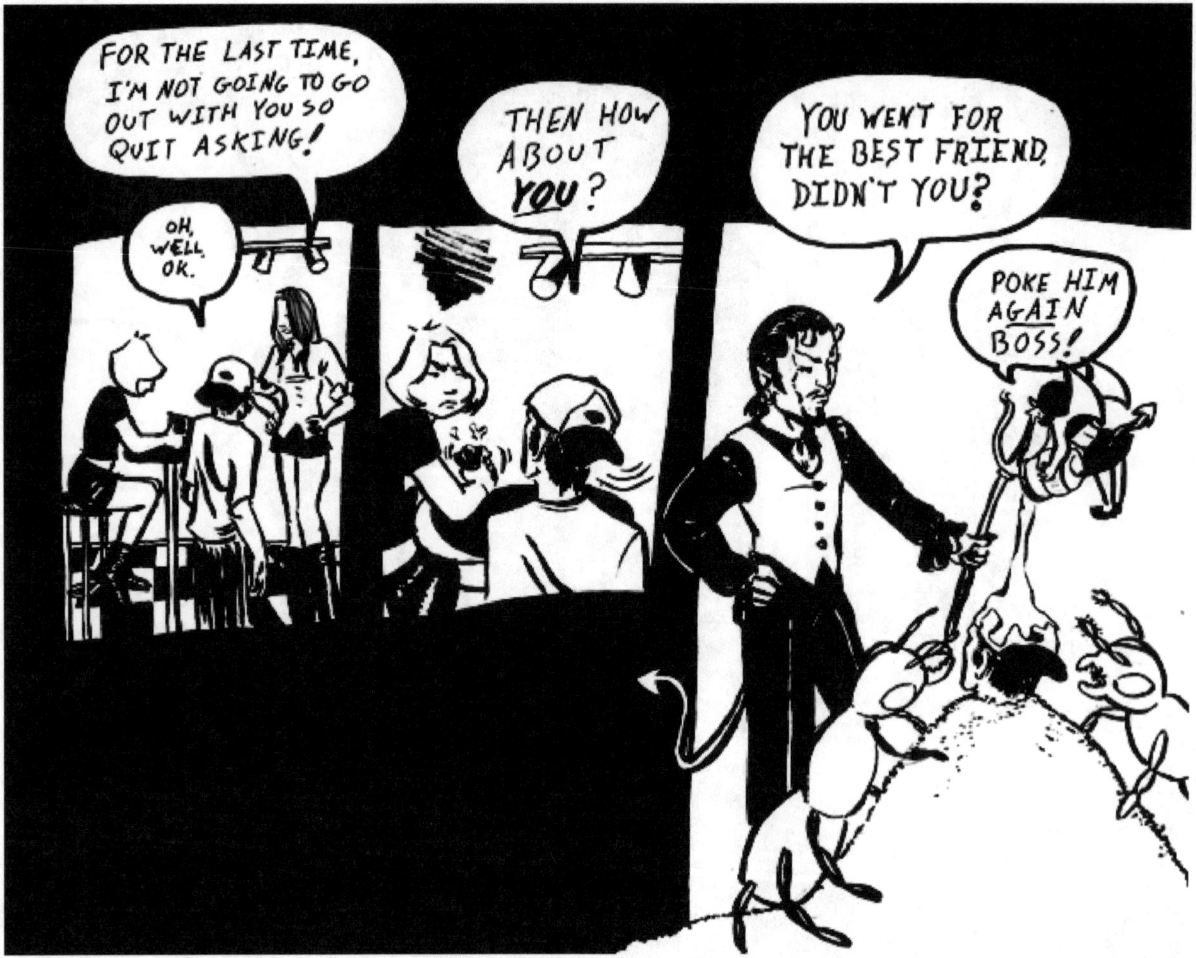
FOR THE LAST TIME, I'M NOT GOING TO GO OUT WITH YOU SO QUIT ASKING!
OH, WELL, OK.
THEN HOW ABOUT YOU?
YOU WENT FOR THE BEST FRIEND, DIDN'T YOU?
POKE HIM AGAIN BOSS!

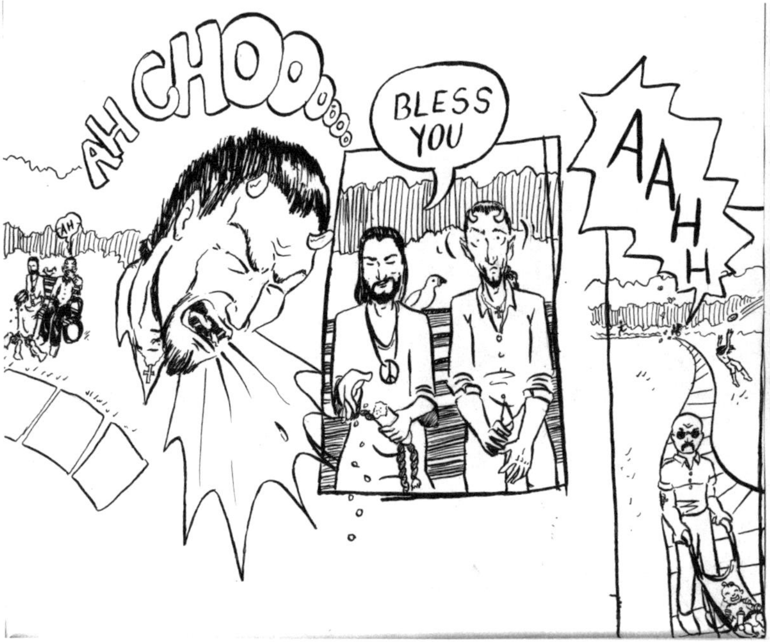
AH
AH CHOOoooo
BLESS YOU
AAAHHH

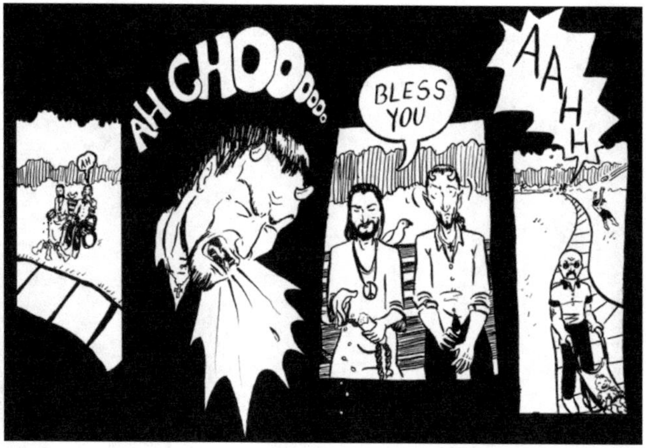
AH
AH CHOOoooo
BLESS YOU
AAHH

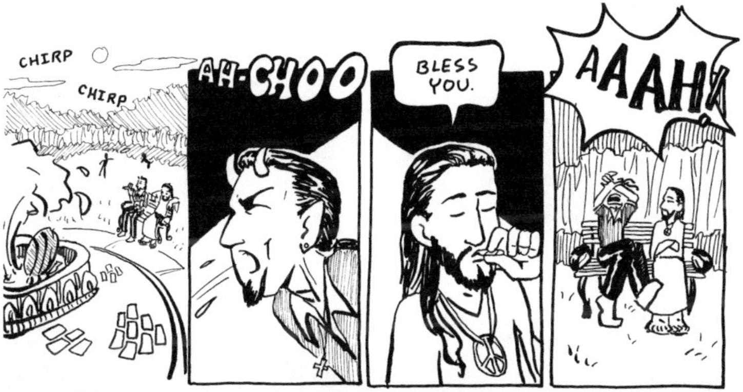
CHIRP
CHIRP
AH-CHOO
BLESS YOU.
AAAH!

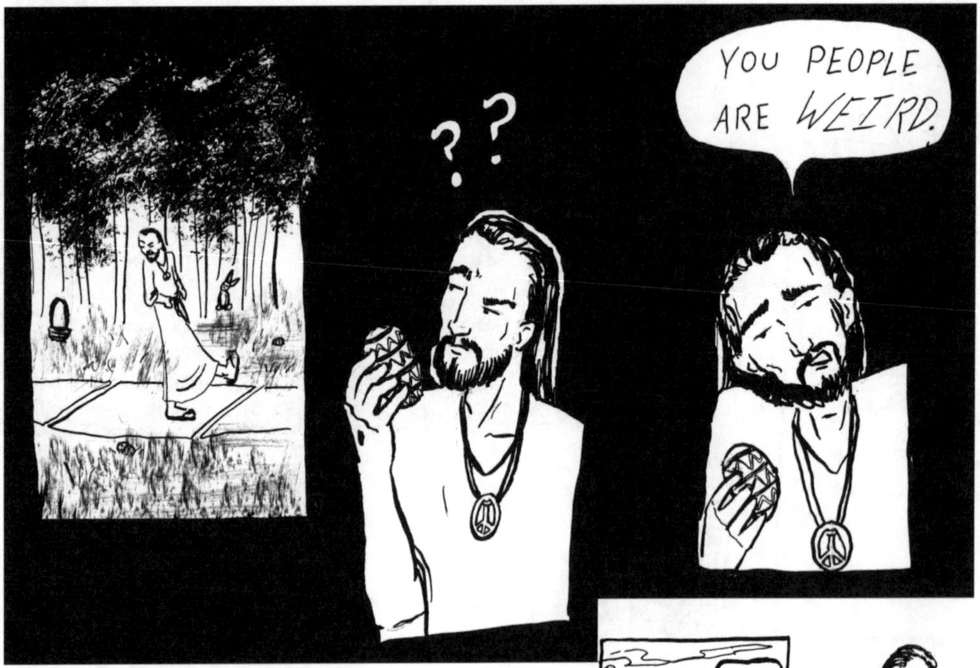
??
YOU PEOPLE ARE WEIRD.

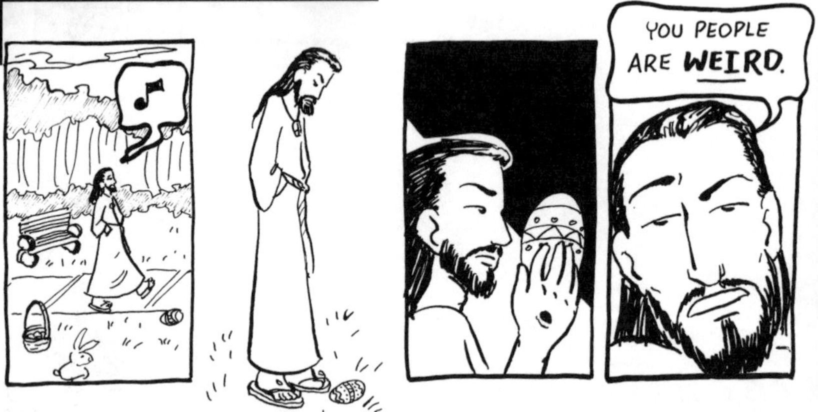
YOU PEOPLE ARE WEIRD.

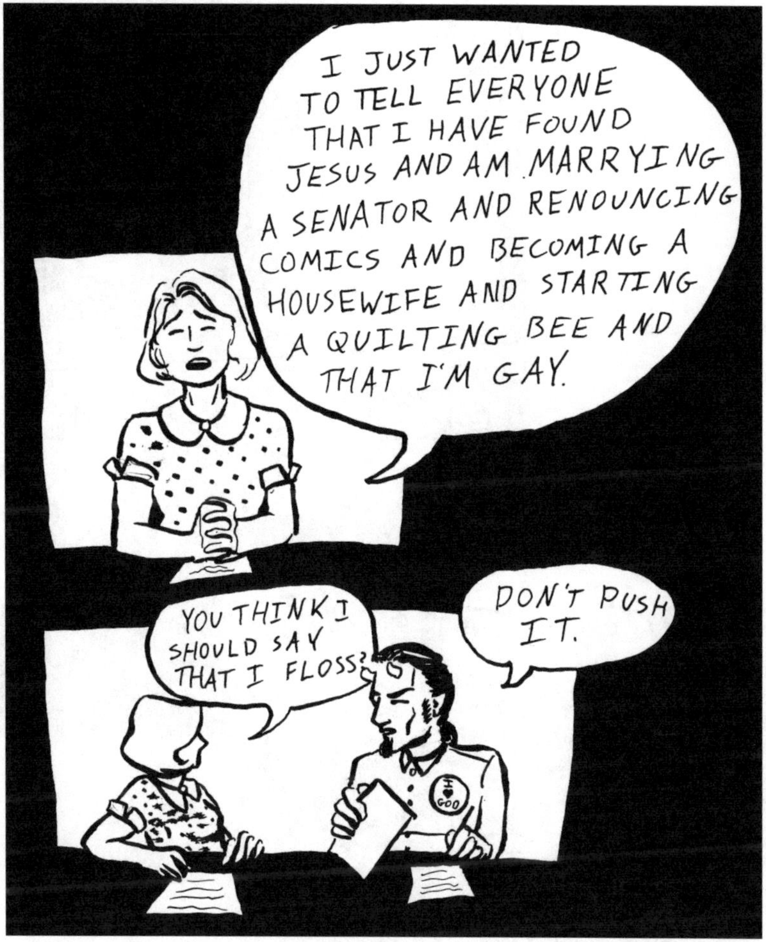
I JUST WANTED TO TELL EVERYONE THAT I HAVE FOUND JESUS AND AM MARRYING A SENATOR AND RENOUNCING COMICS AND BECOMING A HOUSEWIFE AND STARTING A QUILTING BEE AND THAT I'M GAY.
YOU THINK I SHOULD SAY THAT I FLOSS?
DON'T PUSH IT.
I ♥ GOD

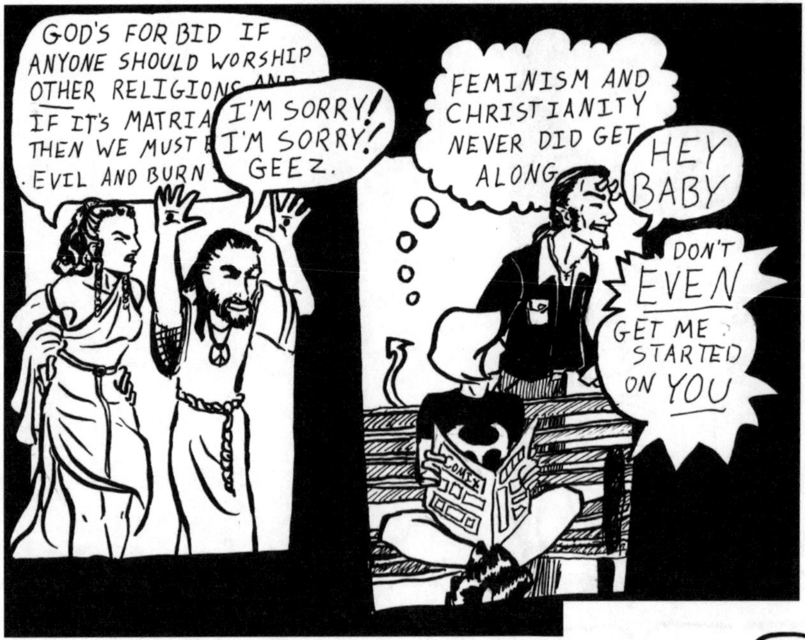
GOD'S FOR BID IF ANYONE SHOULD WORSHIP OTHER RELIGIONS
IF IT'S
THEN WE MUST
EVIL AND BURN
I'M SORRY! I'M SORRY! GEEZ.
FEMINISM AND CHRISTIANITY NEVER DID GET ALONG
HEY BABY
DON'T EVEN GET ME STARTED ON YOU
COMIX

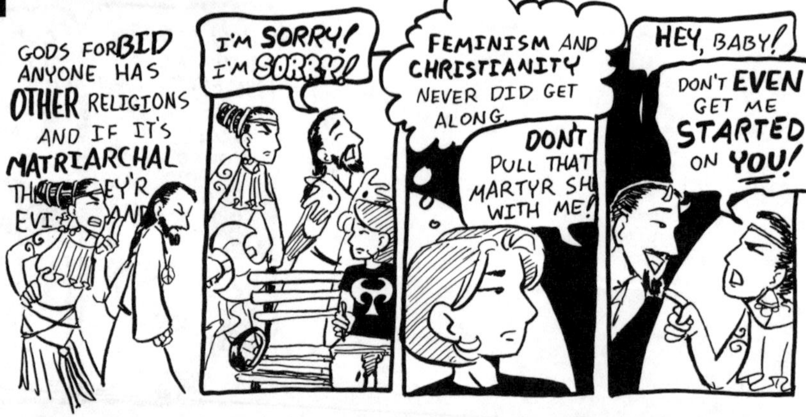
GODS FORBID ANYONE HAS OTHER RELIGIONS AND IF IT'S MATRIARCHAL
I'M SORRY! I'M SORRY!
FEMINISM AND CHRISTIANITY NEVER DID GET ALONG.
DON'T PULL THAT
HEY, BABY!
DON'T EVEN GET ME STARTED ON YOU!

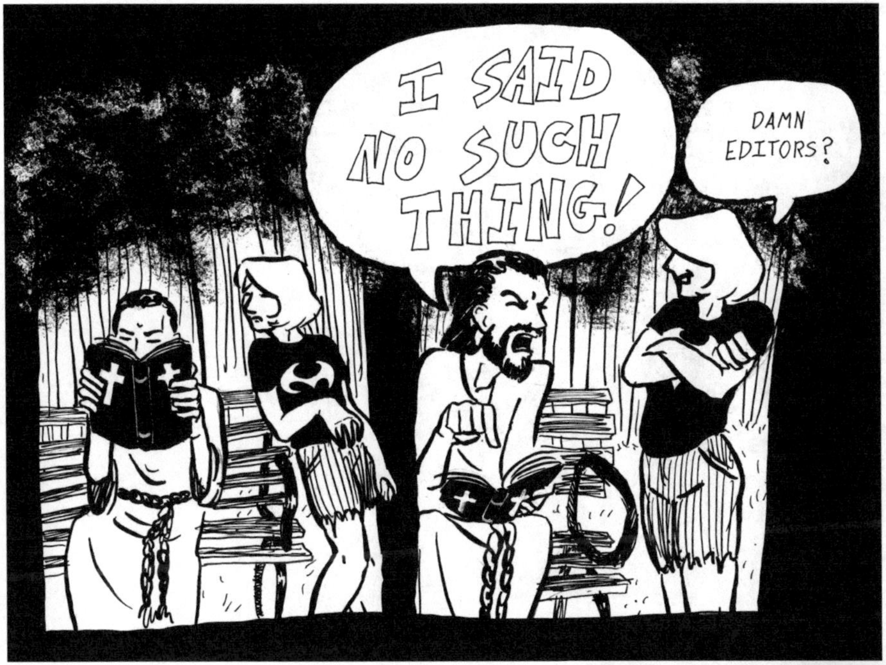
I SAID NO SUCH THING!
DAMN EDITORS?

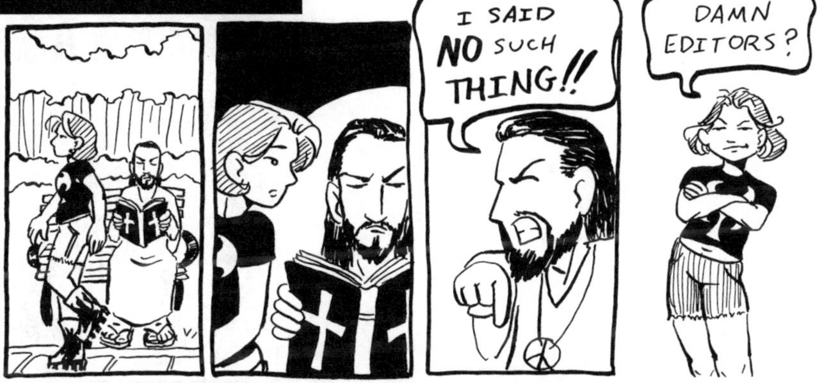
I SAID NO SUCH THING!!
DAMN EDITORS?

www.TheDevilsPanties.com

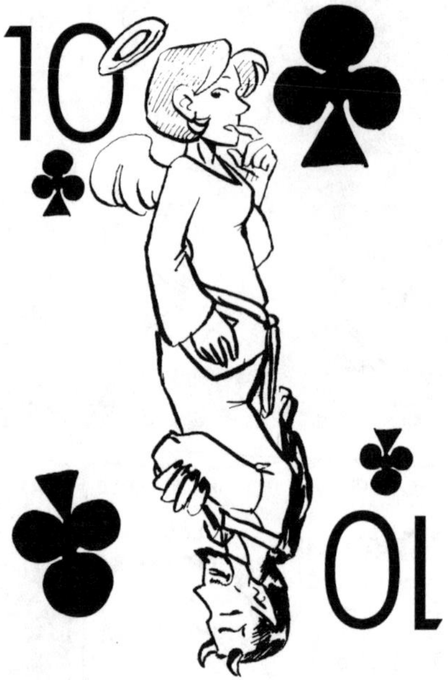

Made in the USA
Columbia, SC
15 August 2024